In the Footsteps of God's Call

A Cuban Pastor's Journey

by

Carlos Alamino

Translated by
Osmany Espinosa Hernández

Edited by
David Peck and Brian Stewart

In the Footsteps of God's Call
A Cuban Pastor's Journey
Copyright © 2008
All rights reserved.

The Spanish edition is entitled
Tras las huellas del llamado
Copyright © 2006 by Carlos Alamino

Translated into English by Osmany Espinosa Hernández

Edited by David Peck and Brian Stewart

Cover design by Christian Stewart

Scripture quotations are from :
Holy Bible: New King James Version. *NKJV*. Copyright © 1982 by Thomas Nelson, Inc. Used by permission. All rights reserved.

ISBN 978-0-615-24440-2

Printed in the United States of America

I dedicate this book to the Lord Jesus Christ, without Whom I would be able to do nothing; to my beloved family; and to all those who in one way or another have given their selfless assistance so that this ministry could carry out His call.

Contents

Acknowledgments 7

Foreword 9

1 I Was Simply Chosen *11*

2 A Divine Revelation: the Vision *23*

3 First Step of Faith: the Mission *27*

4 God's Power Upholds Us *33*

    1) A Death Threat from a Satanic Cult *33*
    2) God Delivers a Woman from Death *36*
    3) Glass Shards in Our Food *41*
    4) Seven Accidents and a Great Deliverance *42*
    5) Accused of Murder *47*
    6) Inocencia: a Desperate Mother *49*
    7) How Pozo Redondo Was Reached . . . *50*
    8) The "Los Muchísimos" Gang . . . *51*
    9) We Have No Food *53*
    10) Two Different Women, Two Different Ways *55*
    11) The Outcasts Become Glorious *56*
    12) Barnardo Can't Read *59*
    13) A Month With No Salary *61*
    14) "Your Son Will Die. We Did All We Could." *62*
    15) A Missionary Trip to Haiti *67*

5 An Important Decision *71*

6 Starting the Bible School *77*

Contents

7 Evangelistic Crusades from East to West *83*

8 Evangelizing Children *89*

9 The Moses Orphans' Program *95*

10 Constructing the Redeemer Baptist Church *99*

11 International Prayer Center *105*

12 Make a "STOP" *109*

Acknowledgments

I thank God — the God of Abraham, Moses, and Jacob; of Joseph and Daniel; of Peter, John, and Paul — for showing Himself in these days as He has always done. His grace and mercy have sustained me. His work, His power, and His faithfulness have given me more than sufficient reason to write this book.

I am grateful to my parents, Arnaldo & América, for being my first Bible teachers and for giving me the example that the Christian life can indeed be lived as God commands. I appreciate their example of constant prayer, their unfailing patience and love, and their understanding of God's call on my life. Thank you, Mom & Dad, for loving me so much. Thanks also to all my aunts, uncles, and cousins.

I praise God for the wife He has given me; she has always been a great blessing. Soledad has lived through every experience mentioned in this book, and not as a spectator, but as a crucial part of everything, working night and day. I am very aware of the great effort she has made in order to meet all of her responsibilities as wife, mother, and church leader. I believe and confess, with all my heart, that my wife is a gift of God for my life.

To my children Carlos and Lianette I express my appreciation for all their affection and support throughout these years of ministry. They have never complained during the times when they had to go without certain comforts in order to meet other needs. They have always looked for ways to please their parents and have been a great help when I needed to get something done. Carlitos and Lianny, thank you for your hugs and kisses. Thank you for inspiring me with your obedience, which has helped change suffering to happiness and sadness to joy.

It is a pleasure to be able to publicly thank our adopted daughter Lisset who has lived among us with great love. Since she was a child she has served us with great responsibility and sacrifice. As a missionary she is also a real example.

I am grateful to the Baptist Church of Babiney, where many of these incidents in the book took place, as well as the churches in Cauto Cristo, La Seis, Limoncito, as well as the many missions we've ministered at. Thank you to The Redeemer Baptist Church in Céspedes, the congregation that God has given me to pastor, for your unconditional love. Thank you Nolaima, Ledys, Armando, Reinaldo, Jorge, Mireya, Leonides, and all of you.

My thanks to Dulce Almaguer for her help with this manuscript, and Nelson Donet for arranging the formatting and printing. I appreciate the direction and encouragement provided by Enio Navarro, President of the Baptist Convention of Eastern Cuba.

I am grateful to Park Cities Baptist Church for their love and support. Thank you pastor Denison, Jeff, Robert, Bob, Uncle Bory and others.

I thank God for my country, for allowing me to be born here, and especially for the rural area of Trilladera where I learned to love the Lord since I was a child.

This book and my ministry in general would not have been possible without all these people I've mentioned, plus many more that space does not permit me to name. Each person has been used by God in His plan, and I am grateful that the Lord has shown me how to work as part of a team.

Foreword

This book is the true account of one man's experience encountering and responding to the call of God on his life. More than simply communicating a biography or testimony, I hope to motivate men and women to rise with determination to respond positively to the call of God.

It has not been easy to recall and completely chronicle the long history of God's faithfulness in guiding my life and ministry. In fact, at times it seemed that putting fallen leaves back on a tree might have been an easier task. The writing of this book has been accomplished at the price of many tears, sleepless nights, and other challenges. The inconvenient and frequent power blackouts common in Cuba made writing with a computer an ordeal, especially when complete pages of text were lost. Gathering and organizing documents and pictures, dusting off old files, and interviewing people who played important roles in this story helped to make the dream of documenting my life as God's servant a reality.

Servant of God, my prayer is that once you have read this book you will be inspired to stay faithful to the Lord, knowing that your work in Him is not in vain. Remember, when the curtain of history closes, only what you have done for God will remain. Throughout time, God has chosen faithful men and women to carry out His work. So, after having accepted the challenge of living for Christ, there is no other option than to serve Him, regardless of the consequences.

I want you to know that a willing heart is the first step in following the footprints that will lead you to do Christ's work.

1

I Was Simply Chosen

On an afternoon in 1954, the old merchant Julio Meneses dropped by the home of my father's parents, León and Obdulia Alamino, in the peasant village of Trilladera, Cuba. He was a peddler, selling clothing door to door. As darkness fell, my grandparents allowed the elderly man to stay in their home overnight. Who could have known that this simple man would bring the Good News to my family? My grandparents received the Lord Jesus Christ as their personal and all-sufficient Savior that day.

From the time of her conversion, my grandmother was a true missionary. Her relationship and experience with God caused her to be a woman of prayer who devoted the rest of her life to intercession, so that her family would believe and serve the Lord Jesus Christ. It is now clear that her prayers were answered. Because of her faithfulness and prayer, she has become a blessing to her children, her grandchildren, and her grandchildren's children.

I was born on December 27th 1961, in Jatibonico, a city in the central region of Cuba, in the days following the revolutionary changes in Cuba and shortly before the Cuban Missile Crisis. I lived my first year at the home of my maternal grandparents. Then, due to economic problems, my family moved to Trilladera, a sparsely-populated town about seven miles away from Jatibonico, to the home of my father's parents. Our arrival further stretched the already crowded conditions of my grandparent's home, as my two uncles and their families were already living there.

According to my parents account, they used to sleep on a bed in the living room. Needless to say, it was a challenge to share these small quarters while attempting to maintain privacy, intimacy, family structure, and to raise their little son appropriately. After a family conference, it was decided that each family would be responsible for their own food, and my grandfather gave each family a small garden plot on which to grow staple food crops, including peanuts, beans and corn.

The over-crowded housing motivated my parents to work towards obtaining their own home. My father worked long hours cutting sugar cane, and my mother rose at 2:00 am to make and sell fritters, all the while saving a little money whenever possible.

God blessed their faith and diligent efforts greatly. One day, they were able to build a humble wooden house with a tile roof and cement floors. The most outstanding thing about the house was the beautiful garden that they had designed and maintained with great passion and care. We were very happy; only three houses were near ours, and our 17 neighbours were members of our extended family.

Trilladera was a very poor place that offered few opportunities and little promise, but right there, in that tiny house, I began my first Bible classes. My parents were my first teachers. My father taught me to live by faith, and my mother showed me that

Family photo taken 1971. My father Arnaldo, mother América, sister Aixa, and me.

we can see victory in the midst of tears and suffering. I am sure that my Christian upbringing began in the heart of my parents before I was conceived. They often told me of the many hours they used to spend in prayer so that their children would remain faithful and committed to the work of the Lord.

As a small boy, I used to take breakfast to my father in the fields; sometimes finding him tilling the land or cutting sugar cane. As I walked the paths to meet him, I could hear the birds sing. I often jumped for happiness or ran trying to catch the birds in my hands. I recall with pleasure my dad wearing a woven straw guano hat, his shirt soaked with sweat, but smiling whenever I came, saying, "God bless you, my son! You are a little man already!" While we ate breakfast together, enjoying the beauty of nature, he told me stories about the Creator, explaining that God existed, that He was the owner of everything, and that He was a God of love who cared about me very much.

Me at 12 years old.

At home, we had family devotions every evening. No matter how tired they were from work, my parents consistently made this time a top priority. During one of these devotions, I received Jesus Christ as my Savior, though I was only five years old. From that day on, they taught me to study and comment on a biblical text, once a week. Sometimes, I would awaken at night and see my parents praying on their knees in front of my bed. When my younger sister Aixa was born, they also prayed fervently for her. These experiences provided training and positively marked my life in such a way that I longed to imitate their example. Although they were never able to give me material wealth, they instilled in my heart the greatest wealth in the world: Jesus Christ.

When I was twelve, we moved back to Jatibonico, where we joined a church fellowship. I was discipled by Pastors Orlirio Llerena and Eumelia Carvajal who treated me as a member of their family. I also thank other teachers from the church, including Mario Felipe, who had a strong, but always encouraging voice and Lucy Quintero, who used to teach us the Bible in a small room in the church. Although we were sometimes scolded, I have pleasant memories of María Abradelo, who directed the youth in drama productions for Christmas, Easter, and other holiday celebrations. These and other faithful saints had great influence on my life during this four- year period. I have high regard and affection for them because God used them as instruments to shape Christian character and faith in me.

At the age of 16, I began working at the Uruguay Sugarcane Mill located in an adjacent town. After an apprenticeship, I became a *pailero* (a welding specialist). This way I was able to help supplement my parent's income and help my sister, who has always been very special to me.

Two years later, I left to fulfil my mandatory military service as a member of the Youth Labor Army. After basic military training, our division began to work the sugarcane fields, cutting cane for transfer to the mill for sugar production. My years of military service were difficult days of hard labor and many sacrifices, and full of sad experiences. I read my New Testament and prayed every night under the trees, as this was the only way I was able to find the strength for each day. The distractions of military life were very difficult for me initially, but my parents encouraged me with a strong admonition, saying, "Plant the flag of Christ upon all things and never lose your faith." My grandmother Obdulia was also an encouragement to me and told me one day, "Fall in love with your job, and it won't seem like work." These words strengthened and encouraged me to labor with all my might. I became one of the ten best workers in the division.

As a reward for my work, I was given some small electric appliances that were needed by my family. During that period, non-essential items were scarce in Cuba, and few Cubans could afford them. I ran home joyfully and gave them to my parents as a gift. I felt great satisfaction and it gave me great pleasure to bless them, because I owed them so much.

When I completed my service to the army, I was sent to work at the Ecuador Sugar Mill, in the province of Ciego de Ávila. While working there, I was in a serious accident. I was hit by a tractor and knocked to the ground. As it drove across my torso and legs, I heard people screaming, "You killed him! You killed him!" I felt no pain or any sensation in my extremities. It was as if my arms and legs had been separated from my body and I had no strength or control over them.

I was vaguely aware of the sound of the ambulance taking me to the Surgical Hospital in Ciego de Ávila, where the staff hastily summoned the surgeons and orthopaedic doctors. I heard the doctors consulting together about an urgent operation. With the little strength that I had left, I said, "Lord, have mercy on your son!" Then I cried out loudly, "Help me, God!" I was placed in a room awaiting surgery. As I waited for the doctors' decision, I began to feel something strange in my body. I felt that my extremities were gaining new life, and I began to feel movement in my arms and legs. I was able to sit up and discovered that I could move my torso and waist. I continued testing my faith and got off the stretcher and began to  walk. I was puzzled, but I was sure that God had performed a profound miracle in me. The doctors were astounded at what they saw. The Lord, in His immense mercy, completely restored my body.

As a youth I played baseball and developed a passion for the sport. I had been part of the youth team of Matanzas and had a very successful and popular amateur career. I felt happy whenever I saw my name in the newspapers and I came to believe that I was important because of my success and skill in the game. It gave me joy and satisfaction when I heard others speak about the great plays I had made in the previous game. In 1979, as an 18 year-old, I was selected to play in the nationwide league. This was an incredible opportunity and a prestigious honour.

When I was packed and ready to leave home for training camp, my father asked me, "Why you don't pray first and ask God what He wants to do with you?" "No," I said, fearing that the Lord would change my plans. I did not want God to hinder what had cost me many years of sacrifice, training, and dedication to obtain. My father persisted until I was convinced, so I left my baggage at the front door and went alone into my room. I knelt down in front of my bed (not completely, just on one knee; with my other leg ready to leave for the Stadium). I had not yet opened my mouth to pray when I was suddenly filled with an overwhelming sadness and began to cry. I hardly understood what was happening as thoughts of family, friends and baseball teammates who did not know Christ flooded my mind. I had never thought of them before, but as I became aware of their need, I felt His voice speaking within my spirit, saying, "They are going to hell because there is no one who would preach to them".

    A strong passion for the lost immediately filled my heart and took control of my life. I understood that God was calling me to do His work. At that very moment, I had a very difficult decision to make. I knew that I was being asked to quit baseball, though it was so important to me. I was called to devote myself fully to the ministry that He had for me. I had been blinded to this call until this time because of my love of baseball and other things that had distracted me.

    From that moment forward I obeyed God's call, left professional baseball and became active in my local church. I served as president of the youth department, a position I held for four years. I also worked as head of the church deacons for a year. I began to be invited to churches to preach as an evangelist, and for a long time thought that this was God's call on my life.

One Saturday, after the weekly youth service, I hurried home to watch the 10:30 p.m. movies on television. They were the best movies of the week, and I watched them faithfully. I went to bed at 2:30 am., but no matter how much I tried to sleep, I could not. I struggled to sleep without any success. Suddenly, I was surprised by the voice of God that audibly spoke to my conscience saying, "Four hours watching TV and never one hour with me". I did all I could to flee from that voice, but three times I heard the same thing; "Four hours watching TV and never one hour with me". Grief flooded my being. It was true, that although I constantly worked for God, I never spent one hour alone with Him. Right there, on my knees, in the middle of the night, I asked him to forgive me and committed to dedicate four hours daily in prayer, examining His Word. In a few days, I felt that my life was beginning to change; I could understand the Bible better and became more sensitive to His voice.

I began to experience what it was like to walk with Christ and to have an intimate relationship with Him. I told Him my secrets, my weaknesses, and knew that He understood me and strengthened me. In the moments that were most difficult, when I was at the point of giving up, He would hear my cry and would deliver me.

I had become engaged to Soledad Matos Legrá shortly after I had finished my military service. Soledad was the daughter of Arildo Matos and Eunice Legrá who served as directors of the Villa Teresita Camp belonging to the Baptist Convention of Eastern Cuba.

On December 3rd, 1982, we were married at the Baptist Church in Jatibonico. After our honeymoon, we went to live in a small house that we built behind my parents' home in Trilladera, where the bed, kitchen, four chairs and a TV set were all together in one room. Everything was humble and simple, but it was ours. We did not even have a table to use, but I felt blessed when I saw Soledad working hard and willing to face every challenge by my side.

In February 1987, I was in Santiago de Cuba where our denomination's annual conference took place. There, a call to pastoral ministry was made and I could not avoid it. The Lord had called me on several past occasions, but I had never made a decision because of some confusion that I experienced. That day I could not resist any longer; so I stood up and went to the platform, where I was prayed for. From then on nothing made more sense in my life than being completely devoted to the sacred calling of pastoral ministry. When I told my wife about it, she said to me in amazement, "I don't want to be a pastor's wife!"

Her response was difficult for me to hear. She had been born into a pastor's home. The history of Soledad's family had always been very hard for her. As managers of the Villa Teresita Camp, Soledad's family had grown up seeing and hearing the challenges and needs experienced by pastors throughout Cuba. Her grandfather, Pastor Victor Manuel Legrá had been the founder of many churches in Maisí, the easternmost area of Cuba. His family had endured very difficult times, as he supported his family of 13 on a wage of only 10 cents per month. Soledad said, "I know what living in a pastor's home is like, almost all the pastors visit this Camp and I'm aware of their sufferings. I am willing to work and to give up everything for His work, but without taking on any pastoral responsibility".

I needed her support, and trusted that the Lord would complete the work He had begun. One night, Soledad had a very deep experience with God and decided to accept the call. My burden was lifted then, because I wanted her to receive a confirmation of His call as well.

Obeying God's call, however, was not easy. I had to face several adversities. My boss refused to accept my resignation from work. One afternoon, my fellow workers made fun of my decision saying, "Repent, God loves you!" roaring with laughter. While this happened, I experienced extraordinary joy because I saw how God had used that moment for me to give them the message of repentance and share His love. Normally, it's forbidden for an employee to talk about God at work, but through that period of ridicule and testing, the message of God was being proclaimed.

After an intense time of prayer, my employer accepted my resignation in September of 1987. I began my studies at the Baptist Seminary in Santiago de Cuba. I dedicated all my days to serve the Lord. During this time, the people of Cuba were undergoing a precarious time of political and national difficulty. Called the "Special Period," there was nothing "special" about it, in the best sense of the word. Rather, it was a time lasting several years where there was a great scarcity of food and basic resources. The collapse of the Soviet Bloc trade support left the economy of Cuba in a crippling and longstanding crisis. Subsidies ceased, factories closed, and food and other shortages were overwhelming. The nation had never seen anything like that before, and times were very hard. And it was precisely at this time that I became a full-time seminary student. Soledad had to quit her work because she did not have anybody who could look after our first son, Carlitos.

The money I had made in my job had been hardly enough to cover food expenses, so any other purchases or needs were simply unobtainable. A few days before leaving for the seminary, we had been at a summer camp. When we returned home, we found that our suitcases with our best clothes and shoes had been stolen, so I had to borrow clothes and receive gifts from the brothers to go to seminary.

I received a monthly student stipend of 105 pesos, approximately $0.55, U.S. dollars. I would send 80 pesos to my wife and keep 25 pesos. This situation forced Soledad to truly depend on God, thus becoming a real servant of the Lord Jesus Christ. She took care of our small son and worked tirelessly during the four long years of my training. In my first year of seminary, I could only visit my family for two days each month, leaving Soledad to place her daily needs before God. God had given me a great woman who was strong, enterprising and courageous. She has always been by my side; she is a real gift from God.

The four-years at the seminary changed and impacted my whole life. Today I thank and honor each professor: Samuel Entenza, Dara Figueras, Félix Perrand, Ester Entenza, Ondina Rosa Alarcón, Ondina Maristany, Rafael Mustelier, Erlinda Mayeta, Gelacio Ortiz, Moraima Guasch, Lilia Lucero, Francisco Álvarez, Joel Rosales, Alvio González Maceo, Helen Black, and Teresa Abella for their affection and special treatment. I can not forget to thank Alfredo, our cook, for his love and care. All of them were used of God to form the character of Christ in me. I will always be grateful to them.

2

A Divine Revelation: the Vision

Upon receiving my degree and pastoral ordination, I began to work as the pastor of a small church in Babiney, a little village located 20 kilometers from Bayamo, the capital city of the province of Granma. I fasted and prayed in the church at 6:00 am, on November 6th 1991. I had been reading the Bible and was seeking God in order to know His will and how I was to work in the village to win lives for Christ, establish outreach missions, and plant new churches. I also sought the Lord for my congregation because the country was going through the most difficult times of the "Special Period." Most families had great economic difficulties, food was scarce, and spiritual occultism prevailed. The Catholic Church was the only church spoken of; and it was on the decline. Atheism was a deeply rooted belief in the culture. Other satanic religions were practiced, including voodoo, witchcraft, and spiritualism. Only one percent of the population indicated interest in the person of Christ or the Christian faith.

As I prayed that morning, God gave me a vision. He showed me a church and a crowd that entered through the main door, leaving through the back door. I then saw many churches and several multitudes that entered and left through the same doors. I was amazed to see that most of the people were young. I heard their conversations after the services were over. They spoke about work, sports, movies and complained constantly. They spoke more about fun than about commitment. They were more concerned about fleshly desires than spiritual growth. Their goal was to possess bicycles, motorbikes, good clothes, and go to the university. Deep within my soul I heard the voice of God saying:

"I will send many people to the churches in the last days. There will be great growth in the Church, but they will leave unchanged because the Church is not prepared to teach the multitudes. Some will remain out of self-interest and religiosity, full of the cares of life, and lost in their own interests. False teachers will come to distort My truth. I am calling out a new generation of young people with a missionary purpose, who are willing to give everything in order to fulfill my Word in Cuba and the nations."

"But, Lord!" I replied, "Why me? I am poor; I live in an insignificant place outside the city. There are others who have better resources, opportunity, and more knowledge." While I was saying this, the vision of the multitudes entering the churches came again, and I heard God's voice saying, "Raise up for Me youth with a purpose!"

That morning, after that time of prayer, I understood that I was being called to make a decision, and I asked God for instruction. A great silence filled the church building. At that time the Holy Spirit revealed to me what was about to begin. What were His purposes? I grabbed a pencil, some paper and under the inspiration of the Holy Spirit I wrote:

1. Train young people to minister for God in Cuba and the nations.
2. Support these workers economically in order to send them to plant new churches.
3. Evangelize children to prepare and strengthen the Church of the future.
4. Spread the Gospel across Cuba through evangelistic crusades from East to West.

I began to have greater insight into the vision that God was showing me. It became clear that that He purposed to develop a ministry which would facilitate the collaboration of churches in developing training for evangelism and church planting, applying solid Biblical and theological teaching in order to satisfy the hunger for the Word that He would develop within Cuba. Thus, the *Ministry of Purpose* began to take shape.

When I began to share this vision and plan with people, many scoffed at the idea, and would not even listen to it. Some said, "How on Earth would you establish a school, support full time missionaries, train children's workers, and organize evangelistic crusades across the whole country under the circumstances we in live today?" In spite of this negative initial response, a group of children and youth, ages 9 to 16, heard and believed what God had revealed to me. They were willing to accept the challenge, no matter what the cost.

Those were very difficult times throughout Cuba. The nation was in an economic crisis. The value of the peso fell to the point that it took around 130 to 150 Cuban pesos to make one US dollar. My monthly salary was the equivalent of 70 US cents. My wife had to cook our food on an open fire. Never before had we lived through so much hardship. At this time of national crisis, every Cuban was forced to focus on basic survival. The hearts and eyes of the country and the Church in Cuba had little vision for more than daily needs.

I was sure God had spoken. The vision was faithful and truthful. Our faith grew as we considered that the God of Abraham, Joseph, Jacob, Moses, Daniel, the apostles and Paul had visited me, giving me the confidence to believe that He who began the work would finish it.

3

First Step of Faith: the Mission

A few days after having received this vision, I decided to begin by faith. We summoned the youth of the church to a morning meeting, and 15 people came. Among the attendees was a first-time visitor, a young woman, Dulce Maria Almaguer, who knew nothing about God.

I started the meeting with prayer, and then explained all that God had revealed to me. I told them, "You are the first young people called to be Youth With a Purpose. You are called to put God's project into practice." I confided in them that I did not have anything to offer them, not even a lunch for the day, but that the Lord Jesus Christ was calling them to be missionaries and teachers of the Bible who would plant new churches, and some would travel the country giving evangelistic crusades throughout Cuba, and then to the nations.

When I explained the vision to them they were very surprised. This group of young adults were without resources, from poor families, but demonstrated a sensitivity and willingness to serve the Lord. A very special atmosphere developed as the group was moved to prayer on our knees. I recall that we lost track of time as we prayed, where a steady and sincere petition was raised. A chorus of voices, sometimes quietly and sometimes with strength and power were united in spirit, saying, "Here we are Lord, we surrender all to You. We are willing to do Your will. Use us in the way You want!"

At noon, a sister told me, "Pastor, there's no food for lunch." I replied, "God is in control, let's believe He'll provide." Some minutes later the answer came. A brother from the church brought our family a pastoral gift of a 30 to 40 pound pig that he had raised. At this same moment, a truck loaded with bananas broke down on the highway across from our church and the driver told me, "I'd like to give you some fruit because it is already ripe and will soon go bad." In this way the Lord showed His power and confirmed that He would support the ministry that had just begun.

After eating, more hours passed as the young people remained on their knees in prayer. We experienced the call and assurance of God in power. We felt His love, His affection and were wrapped in His arms. It was then that Dulce Maria was touched by the Lord Jesus Christ and received Him as her only Savior. She left that place changed and filled with the calling of God on her life, and became a missionary who has never failed God or the ministry, despite having walked through the darkest of valleys.

That evening, it was decided that we should begin a school to train those first young men and women as church planting missionaries, and this became the focus of our energy. With happiness in our hearts, we found a place to meet, though it was only a spot beneath the trees with the branches and sky as a roof for this first classroom. There were 15 students; dreamers filled with hope who believed the call on their hearts, willing to face the challenge that those difficult times would produce.

The youth doing an outreach in Babiney in 1992.

As the ministry training began, we taught the students the priority of being willing to carry out the evangelistic mission. God prepared me in a special way to be able to teach on these topics. From the time God began to move through this ministry, it seemed that every book and all Biblical materials I received dealt only with the topic of missions and church planting. I studied the history of missions in Cuba and the lives of our predecessors who brought the Gospel to Cuba. I was particularly impacted by the life of Cuban evangelist Victor Manuel Legrá, my wife's grandfather.

I took the opportunity to visit Pastor Legrá's house in the tiny village of Old Town, at Maisí, the country's easternmost area. I opened a forgotten trunk that was covered with dust; perhaps untouched since his death. I found his notes, books and messages there, written in his own hand. Each sermon had a salvation call. I was assured by his family that whenever he spoke, he presented an altar call so that people could receive Christ as their Savior.

My visit to this godly man's home marked the beginning of a walking evangelism tour in the mountains that lasted 23 days. We traveled 5 to 10 kilometers every night, walking through remote mountainous places, visiting small villages and homes. I was encouraged by the writing of Pastor Legrá, who explained that many lives could be won to Christ, and that big difficulties were not a reason to stop faithfully presenting the missionary message. The fields were ready for the harvest, and many men would be needed who were willing to pay the price of service; those who would keep in mind the urgent need and opportunity for evangelism in Cuba. Pastor Legrá's example of sacrifice became a standard for us. If Victor Legrá had chosen to work for a salary instead of giving himself completely to the spread of Christ's message, none of the many churches that began as a result of his ministry would have been established, as there were no organizations or individuals to offer financial support for the work of an evangelist in Cuba. These experiences motivated us to carry on with the Church Planter Training School. Although there was no money, there were men and women of faith willing to make this vision a reality.

Along with the Church Planter Training School we initiated rallies and training entitled, *Youth With a Purpose: Cuba for Christ and the Nations*. We would gather 100 to 200 youth, present the challenge of serving God in missions, train and disciple those who were willing to make a commitment, and send them where the Gospel had not been preached. Through this slow process, the hearts of many Christian youth were dedicated and prepared to advance the Gospel in Cuba. We faithfully prayed for specific towns in Cuba and for the nations.

These meetings would be held every six months in different locations throughout Cuba. We often got together at Baptist camps such as Palmarón in Granma and Villa Teresita in Céspedes, Camagüey. Sometimes, we rented secular leisure resorts to hold these activities to accommodate the ever increasing number of youth who attended each meeting. One of these sites was at San German, where the Baptist church is still located. Rev. Abel González was the pastor there at that time. He and Pastor Obed Morales served as two of the lecturers for the conferences. They are still my brothers and partners in ministry, having played an important role in the success of these events.

Three years later, these brothers accompanied me on walking tours to places where the Gospel had never been preached. We visited remote towns, sometimes by bicycle or horse cart. At times we had to spend the night wherever we could find a place, and frequently slept on the ground by the roadside. We were often threatened by satanic sects. We suffered from headaches and weakness due to hunger and thirst, but we went through it with joy because we were fulfilling the command of the Lord: "Go therefore and make disciples of all the nations, baptizing them in the name of the Father and of the Son and of the Holy Spirit, teaching them to observe all things that I have commanded you; and lo, I am with you always, even to the end of the age". (Matt. 28:19-20).

I remember an 84 year-old man named Evelio Figueredo who we met on one of our walking tours. He had an extensive ulcer on his leg and hadn't been able to walk for 40 years. The wound was infested with insects and infection. One day he came for prayer and we anointed him with oil and prayed believing that God would heal him. A few days later, we all saw and rejoiced in the miracle of God's healing. His leg was made whole. His family glorified the name of the Lord for the healing of this 40 year-old illness. He became a faithful supporter of the work, always concerned about our mission trips. Brother Figueredo often used his horse cart to transport us to areas of ministry. We traveled joyfully in the satisfaction of being able to serve the Lord.

Youth With a Purpose meeting, 1996.

4

God's Power Upholds Us

The Gospel continued spreading in the midst of struggles and persecution. God showed His power and authority through each difficulty. Reaching difficult places with the Gospel gave strong evidence of the transforming power of Jesus Christ through the Holy Spirit. Day after day, as we stood against evil with the light of God's Word and witnessed His transforming work in changing lives, we encountered terrifying incidents in the families of the people we used to minister to, and we had to depend totally on God's power for safety and deliverance. The experiences narrated in this chapter demonstrate God's power and support in the midst of the circumstances we encountered while fulfilling the call and obeying God's Word.

1) A Death Threat from a Satanic Cult

When our congregation was getting ready to celebrate Christmas in 1991, I was sent a note that read: "Pastor, if you dare to come preaching around our neighborhood, we will kill you." The note was signed, "The Grave Robbers." Our brothers from the church explained that there was a local satanic cult, nearly 800 strong, who were considered powerful and feared by everyone in the area. As an initiation rite, cult members were required to exhume graves and take cadaver bones. The bones were crushed and fragments placed within open cuts in the skin of cult members. The wounds were then stitched closed, signifying their covenant with the devil. Immediately I was advised not to go into that area. I asked the Lord for guidance in prayer, and was reminded of the story of David and Goliath. I got up from my knees, grabbed my Bible and told the brothers, "Pray for me because I'm going there — in the name of Jesus Christ."

As I was walking in their neighborhood, looking for opportunities to share the Gospel, I was suddenly approached by four men with clubs in hand. I was afraid, but I trusted the power that upheld me. They came within three feet of me and stopped without saying anything. Without stopping, I said "Hello there!" They gave no answer, so I walked on. I shared the Gospel at many homes and some people received Christ. Before returning home, I visited a place where a group of satanic priests were gathered for cultic ceremonies. I did not fully understand why they were meeting there, but I told them about the love of Jesus Christ and invited them to come to the church service.

During the Christmas service on December 25th, after a beautiful drama was enacted, I was preaching. 18 Satanists came to the service and stood at the door. Their head priest was with them, standing in the center of the open doorway. There was great fear throughout the building. I closed my eyes and began to pray for them. As I prayed, I could hear footsteps coming closer to the altar. I heard someone cry out, and opening my eyes saw Thomas, the Satanist leader standing in front of me. I asked him if he was the head priest, but he did not answer.

"Why are you crying?" I asked him.

"Who is your god? Who is your god?"

"Why do you want to know?" I asked.

"Your God is stronger than mine, I know that already."

"What makes you think that my God is stronger than yours?"

"When we got near you to beat you to death, we felt there was something around you that prevented us form harming you; that proved to me, for the first time in my life, that there is a God more powerful than my god. I want to know your God."

"It is possible for you to know Him! He has mercifully brought you here today so that you may repent of your sins and open up your heart to receive Him as your only Savior. He can give you the joy that you've never had. Would you like to make that decision now?"

Thomas fell on his knees in great distress in front of the meeting and asked God to forgive him. The others from his group did the same. As a result, the cult gang that had caused such fear in the area has now completely broken up.

Shortly after his conversion, this former cult leader told us that while he worked for Satan, many people had sought his help to solve their problems. Although he possessed significant supernatural power, it came at a great price. Once, a desperate husband asked to have his hospitalized wife healed from a serious disease. Thomas prepared an amulet for her, offered it to Satan and the sick woman was healed right away. Following this, however, his own wife was seriously burned in an accident.

On another occasion, Thomas had used satanic power to save a girl's life. The next day, his own young daughter was hit by a car; resulting in her becoming permanently crippled. The devil offered Thomas power, but took much of his life in return. Woe is he who is a slave of the devil! Satan does not really prosper people, and if it appears that he does, it's only for a time, and a price must later be paid. Thomas had this kind of experience. When he was released out of his bondage and became free; Christ broke his chains and gave him a new life, eternal life

Following Thomas' conversion and the end of the satanic stronghold in that area, people began to visit the pastor to seek solutions to their needs. The church became the place where they could find comfort and answers. People learned to fear the God because of the reality of that victory.

"The Spirit of the Lord is upon Me, because He has anointed Me to preach the gospel to the poor. He has sent Me to heal the broken hearted, to proclaim liberty to the captives and recovery of sight to the blind to set at liberty those who are oppressed; To proclaim the acceptable year of the Lord." (Luke 4:18-19)

2) God Delivers A Woman From Death

As narrated by my wife, Soledad Matos

On December 19, 1992, I had spent the early morning in prayer and studying the Bible. My son was at school and my husband was at the seminary, so I was alone at home. Around 9:00 am somebody knocked at the door. I opened to a young woman in great distress standing in front of me. I recognized her as the wife of a prominent witch doctor. A few days earlier we had visited the home of her mother, and learned information about this young woman who knew the Lord and at one time had attended an evangelical church. The girl faced very difficult times and a sad situation as the strong and evil spiritual influence of her husband held her in bondage and abuse. She believed that only God's power could set her free from the bondage, but she was afraid to leave her husband. In the past, she had attempted to escape, but demons had told her husband where to find her. This had happened repeatedly, but she decided to seek refuge in our home.

Two days earlier she had once again decided to escape. She left her house and did not return home that evening. Her husband had traveled to a nearby town to attend an idolatrous celebration on the eve of Saint Lazarus' day (December 17th). She had not taken any of her belongings as she fled across the fields to avoid being seen by anyone who would let her husband know of her whereabouts. She almost fainted as she came into my home. She had walked more than 18 miles through fields and open land to avoid being seen, having traveled continuously for nearly 24 hours. Her feet were bare and injured, her legs were bleeding and she was near exhaustion from the heat, her long journey, and from fear. I only had only enough time to get some water and cotton wool to clean her wounds and offer her some hot coffee to raise her low blood pressure when there was another knock at the door.

I opened the door to her husband, knife in hand with another man menacingly standing before me. When I saw them, I asked, "What are you doing here?"

"I've come to kill my wife."

"Who told you your wife was here?"

"I knew she was coming last night. I was told and I know she's here."

"Who is this other man who has come with you?"

"He's my friend."

"Tell your friend that he must leave. He's not needed here."

As soon as the second man heard my words, he immediately left (to the glory of God) without further comment. I was trembling with fear, but I didn't want him to realize that, so I kept praying to God for help and strength. I needed wisdom and discernment to manage this situation as my mind was blocked and filled with anxiety. I worried that this demon-possessed man could take his wife's life in my own house.

I knew that it was very unlikely that I would be able to find anyone in the neighborhood to assist me at that time of the day, as everyone was at work and our house was not on a well-traveled road. I did not worry much about getting help though, as I felt God was directing me to deal with this problem myself. An unusual boldness stirred within me as I watched the husband's friend walk away, and I knew that God was already in control. I did not want the husband to know that we were alone in the house, so I told him, "You may come in, but, first you must leave that knife out here in the porch!"

"I'm going to kill her. She knows she can't leave, and she can't fool me."

"In the name of Jesus, I command you to drop that knife!"

I felt God anointing and emboldening my words with strength and power as I spoke. I walked towards him and repeated, "In the name of Jesus, I command you to drop that knife!" I seized him by the arm and made him drop it. He threw it out in the garden without opposing me. He was reeking, dirty, and unkempt. I dragged a chair onto the porch for him to sit on. God revealed to me that he might have an extra knife or weapons hidden somewhere, so I continued, "Now get rid of everything you have in your pockets and on your body and throw it away." I also commanded him to get rid of all the necklaces, chains, bracelets, and amulets that he wore, using the name of God and claiming His authority over this man and the present evil.

Then the husband told me, "There's something I can't get rid of."

"Why?" I inquired.

"Because it's quite deadly and I can't throw it away. It cost me a great deal and is very important. Besides, it's bewitched so I can't leave it in your back yard. It's very dangerous."

I commanded him again to take it out. It was powder from a dead person's bones that he obtained from a cemetery. He had dug a corpse out, took a bone from the head, grated it and used the powder for witchcraft. He said he had one last thing to do to increase his power.

"What is it?" I asked.

"I must sacrifice a child." He revealed that he had spent the previous three days away from home preparing for this murderous atrocity.

Slowly and reluctantly he dropped everything he had. He took off his shirt, his shoes and his socks. I told him to empty the pockets of his pants. When I was sure he had nothing else in his pockets, I told him,

"Your wife is here, but you need to know that this is the house of the servants of God and you have no power here. Now, in the name of Jesus, I command you not to respond to any satanic order. God grants me the authority to make decisions on your behalf."

As he came in the house, he said,

"Listen, they are laughing at me. They want to come in." There were many satanic powers present where he had left his possessions. They were mocking and tormenting and calling to him. I said to him, "Don't be afraid of them. They can't come in here. This is a Godly place so their power is limited."

I cannot explain everything the Lord showed and allowed me to do during this period, but I could feel His authority, His power, and the strength He gave me as He controlled this man. Shortly before, this man had been ready to murder, but was now growing weak and his strength was leaving him. I rebuked him saying, "Look at your wife. She is in a very poor state and it's all your fault."

His wife was sobbing uncontrollably, bruised, exhausted and terrified. I commanded him to sit in a corner of the living room. "Stay there and do not move." He followed my directions and then asked for some water. I was concerned that he might use this as a way to distract me and attack his wife. I looked outside for someone to draw water for me, because the water supply in the house was gone. Water would have to be retrieved from a neighbor's house. I took a pitcher and six metal cups and quickly went to the backyard. I quietly called out to a Christian neighbor who lived next door and requested some water. While I was doing this, I occasionally threw a metal cup into the kitchen, in order for the man to think I was still inside.

Although this now seems like a ridiculous thing to have done, God had actually kept him still. When the neighbor brought the water I told her, "Please, go home and pray. The man in my house is demon-possessed and I'm going to minister to him." I took no more time to tell her what was going on.

Returning to the house, I sat by his side and started to talk to him. I asked him to tell me the details of all he had done for the last two days. I realized he was unresponsive, his eyes glassy and opened widely, as though he were daydreaming. I began to pray quietly. As I prayed, a demon attacked him, violently strangling him. I had never seen anything like that. The man was tossed across the room, repeatedly knocked to the floor, and beaten. The man was unable to escape as he was strangled and choked, though he fought desperately. It seemed that a war had started. I continued to pray quietly, convinced that God was delivering him, not only from this demon, but from legions of demons. I spent nearly two hours interceding for him. As I prayed, the demons pressed hard upon his chest, stomach, organs and his legs, causing incredible pain. His legs became twisted, he foamed at the mouth and finally when the demon left him, he appeared half dead and unconscious on the floor.

After that, I started praising God with spiritual songs. The man regained consciousness half an hour later, stood up and asked me, "What has happened?" I answered, "The Lord Jesus Christ has set you free! You are a free man now." When he saw his wife, he hugged her and they both cried for a while. All this happened before noon. I told him, "Here's a towel and some clean clothes. Go to the bathroom, shave that dirty beard off and wash that stench of blood and herbs off you." While he was taking a bath, I burned all of his old belongings. Afterwards, I fed them and they slept at our home. They returned to spend New Years with us.

Unfortunately, some months later, he left his wife and returned to his former lifestyle, lacking the self-control to resist sin. His present state now is worse than the first, for as the Bible says; "When an unclean spirit goes out of a man, he goes through dry places, seeking rest; and finding none, he says, 'I will return to my house from which I came.' And when he comes, he finds it swept and put in order. Then he goes and takes with him seven other spirits more wicked than himself, and they enter and dwell there; and the last state of that man is worse than the first." Luke 11:24-26

Eventually he was committed to a mental institution and has remained there, with no family, no faith, no God, and no hope. Sometime later his wife met a Christian man who served the Lord through music ministry. They both serve the Lord now, and enjoy children who are a great blessing to their home.

3) Glass Shards in Our Food

One Sunday morning, my wife rose early and prepared our Sunday dinner before we went to Sunday school. After she made lunch, she left the pot on the stove and we walked over to the church. The kitchen area of our house was in an unsecured area, and was accessible to those passing by.

I remember that worship service, as Soledad played the piano at church. Some sisters looked after our daughter, Liannette, who was 2 years old, while Carlitos sang every song, and prayed aloud. Our church loved to praise the Lord and rejoiced in the worship service. After we concluded, we greeted one another joyfully and began to return to our homes.

Our kids were hungry, so they helped themselves to lunch while we were still talking to some brothers. Later, when we began to eat, I bit something sharp and gritty that hurt my mouth. "It's glass!" I shouted. My wife quickly checked the soup for more glass and found many more pieces. Someone had wanted to harm us, placing crushed glass in our soup while we were away. We watched our children with concern all day, and Praise God, they never suffered any trouble. Whoever had tried to hurt us, had not considered that God is the keeper of our lives and always watches over us. This attempt to destroy us helped increase our trust in Him, and was an encouragement to our congregation, as well. We were reminded that we were facing spiritual warfare, and that the Lord was giving us absolute victory in our safety. We grew in the confidence that nothing could beat the power of our Lord Jesus Christ! This experience was a long-lasting reminder to thank God for his deliverance.

4) Seven Accidents and a Great Deliverance

The Baptist church at Babiney where we served was a happy place in December 1995, as Christmas festivities were being planned. We decided to celebrate Jesus' birth by doing something that would provide every person in town an opportunity to celebrate and enjoy our Savior's birthday. We wanted heaven to rejoice too, so we organized an evangelistic crusade, trusting that many people would offer Jesus their hearts. We understood that whenever a sinner repented, there was celebration in heaven.

This town had been subjected to Satan's power for many years. Because of tradition and their unbelief, some Christians sought help from people who used healing gifts that denied God's power. December was a month of celebration for Christians as well as for the Satanists. December 4th and 17th are celebrations of Saint Barbara and Saint Lazarus, two idols whose celebrations include food offerings, rituals to contact the dead through séances and mediums, and other pagan observances. While some people in town were getting ready for these pagan celebrations, the church was praying for our Gospel crusade so that every family would experience the awesome power of God.

Finally, the day anticipated by every believer in town came. A crusade was not a common event and everyone was anxious to see what would happen. On the first night, there was not enough room for the people in the small church. Many met Christ and others were healed. We witnessed several wonders and miracles.

The next day, the things that happened in the Babiney crusade became the talk of the entire province, and a platform had to build a in the street to accommodate all the people who came for the services. Hundreds of people came for prayer. Thousands gathered on the next night. People came from many areas and even from the capital city of the province. Many sick people were brought from hospitals by their relatives who rented buses and cars to bring them to the crusade believing that God was going to work miracles for their healing.

As the town was rejoicing at the wonders that were happening day by day, some people resorted to devious means and trickery, trying to stop that manifestation of God's power. However, His presence, His lordship and His authority were enough to overcome every challenge from the enemy.

All of this was accomplished without my direct involvement or participation in the meetings. Just as the final plans were being completed for the crusade, I had to urgently travel 497 miles to Havana to obtain a car that we had bought. My parents asked Brother Reinaldo Fajé, an experienced driver to come with because I did not drive much.

On our way home, Brother Fajé was not able to drive. He told me, "I just can't drive, I don't know what's going on." I was forced to take full responsibility for the long drive myself. I committed myself to the hands of the Lord, took the wheel and started driving. We felt fearful along the way, but we did not know why. When we had driven 93 miles, one of the front wheels came off the car. Thank God I was able to control the car, which suffered almost no damage. After fixing the wheel, we drove on. A little farther along, having not slept for the previous two nights, I fell asleep at the wheel. We drove off the road over an embankment and crashed into a streambed that had almost no water. After the shock of the accident, we realized that we were alive and completely unhurt. We felt like laughing and hugged each other. Brother Fajé asked me, "Did you see it?" But I had not seen anything. Then he described with amazement what he had just seen. "When we were falling, I saw two hands holding the car and placing us in the stream, saving us from getting hurt." We praised God for His deliverance. We continued to feel uneasy and nervous though, and did not know what to do.

We sent for a tow truck and were able to continue our trip. When we had gone 37 more miles, we felt a sudden bang and the car careened into the ditch by the road. Again, we were unhurt. We checked the car and realized that it had a steering problem. Though we were very tired and had not eaten anything, we kept driving at a slow speed in order to reach Las Tunas, the next province, where we hoped to find some help.

As we drove past a bus stop, a grey-haired man asked us for a ride. Brother Fajé explained that we could not take him on because the car was having mechanical problems. We pulled away and drove just 30 yards before I sensed God directing me to go back and pick up this man. I stopped, got out of the car and went over to him saying, "God says you're a mechanic and you're going to help me out. Here are the car keys." He was astonished and didn't understand what was happening.

"How did you know I'm a mechanic?" He asked. I explained that God had revealed it to me. Actually, that man was a great mechanic. He took us to his house, discovered and fixed the problem with the car, and even fed us. His name was Suñol.

We left Las Tunas to go to Bayamo, about 43 miles away. We expected nothing else would happen, but without warning, a bull ran onto the road, charged furiously and crashed into our car. Although we were shaken, we were unharmed and the car continued to run.

We traveled on until the engine caught fire. We quickly got out of the car, shouting for help. I burnt my hands trying to put out the fire, while bystanders brought some dirt and put the fire out. I did not have any more strength and dropped flat onto the road, saying, "Lord, that's it; I can't go any further!"

I felt the need to call my wife. A truck had stopped to assist us, so I asked them to take me to the nearest town. Once I was able to contact my wife, I asked her about the crusade. She joyfully told me, "Many awesome things are taking place; more than 1000 people have been evangelized, some spiritualism centers are closing and getting rid of their idols. We have a room full of pagan shrines for you to burn when you come back." When I heard this, the cause of all my accidents in the past 48 hours became clear. Spiritual warfare was affecting our trip. It seemed that the devil was mad and wanted to kill me, but God did not allow him to. I am sure that Satan did not want me to make it home because he intended to keep his idols working. I said to my wife, "Please, gather the church leaders and burn all the pagan shrines immediately." Later that day I told her about all that had happened during my trip.

The church leaders made a large fire and started burning all the idols and fetishes that the new converts had given up. While this was happening, Gabriel Almaguer, (fondly called "the great" because of his willingness to serve) and his son Vladimir came to pick me up in a car. When they arrived, they checked the charred engine. They discovered that when two wires were put together the engine would start. We started the car and returned home without any difficulty. Our problems were over, and I was able to get home at last.

That was an unforgettable week! It was the first time I had ever seen so many people gathered to seek God in one place. I remember one night when huge crowds had come to hear the Word presented. After the service, many did not realize the meeting had ended. The anointing of God was still among the people, the Lord was performing many miracles and healings, and people continued to be converted late into the evening. After the service finished that evening at 11 pm, I was exhausted. I sat in a chair in our living room, leaning back with my eyes closed. Not long before midnight, I heard a car stop and a brother called out to me, "Pastor! Pastor! A bus full of people has just arrived to hear the gospel and be prayed for." I stood up and told those near me, "Come on, the Lord needs us. Open the church."

On greeting the newcomers, I was told they had come all the way from Bayamo. I still cannot not forget a woman whose sons had brought her because she could not walk. Her legs had been burned and the scarring had caused her toes to grow together and her feet to be deformed. As we prayed, God separated her toes and smoothed the taut and scarred skin on her feet and legs. She walked independently back to her seat. These types of experiences were repeated day after day, and the impact they made on me marks the beginning of a transition in our ministry. I saw things occur during those days that I had never expected, and was assured repeatedly that God was sovereign, doing what He wanted, in the ways He chooses.

All the accidents and difficult experiences that happened during this time helped our faith grow, and led us in developing a closer relationship with God. Whenever God is at work, the enemy strives to destroy it. However, we, his children, can have confidence in the Lord as our Shepherd.

5) Accused of Murder

Groups of young adults often met at our church for praise and worship services. Many would travel by bicycle, often coming from considerable distances in order to fellowship and learn more of God's Word together. In 1996, we were holding regular meetings for the youth, who were responding with peaceful enthusiasm and a growing knowledge of God's Word. The enemy never rested though and set a trap that hurt people deeply.

One Sunday evening, the youth arrived on their bicycles. The service began and we were filled with God's presence as we began praising Him. All seemed well, and I presented a message to the group. At the end of my preaching, I was overcome with a sudden illness, high fever, severe pain and trembling weakness that was so overwhelming that I was unable to stand. Some brothers took me home and stayed with me.

As I lay at home, I could not have imagined what was about to take place on the road. The young people who had attended the service were returning to their homes in the moonless night. The road was pitch black and in the darkness, the travelers could not even see those riding with them. Suddenly, a young man, biking in the opposite direction crashed into them. He fell off his bike, striking his head on the pavement. He lay unconscious with a head injury. He was taken to a local hospital and then immediately transferred to the main hospital in Bayamo, Granma, where he died.

To our surprise, we discovered that this young man, a new convert, was known to us. His name was Peter, but had not been at the meeting that evening because he had allowed his non-Christian friends to convince him to go to a party. My wife had visited his home that afternoon and Peter had told her that these friends had lent him a bicycle, and that he felt obligated to go with then. He intended to return early in order to attend the services. Peter's friends reported that he had not enjoyed himself at the party. He had wanted to leave, but no one wanted to come back to town with him. When He saw that it was past 11 pm, he decided to return to town alone. Of course, no one ever expected that he would die.

With tears in their eyes, his friends told me, "Pastor, we made fun of Peter because He was a Christian. Whenever he left his house to go to church we would call to him, saying, 'You are not a man if you don't come and party with us!' So this time he came to the party to prove he was a man."

Such disobedience had caused his death. On that night, when the evidence was collected and witness statements made, I was accused of killing Peter. Peter's grandmother, who was involved in witchcraft, alleged that I had intentionally hit Peter with my motorcycle. Later, false witnesses were presented who testified they had heard Peter cry out, "Pastor, don't kill me! Pastor, don't kill me!" It caused great confusion and difficulty for us, but God had gone before us to vindicate me. He allowed me to become very sick in bed, surrounded by many witnesses who had taken care of me. This fact helped clarify that when the accident happened I was sick at home. I was interviewed by the police, but they finally confirmed my innocence.

The devil had planned to destroy me again because I was hindering his plans, but God, who is powerful, had perfectly worked everything out. Many people were coming to know Christ daily; destroying their shrines and establishing new home church fellowships. God timed my sickness to come that night so that my innocence would be obvious. God's Word is true: "…He who is in you is greater than he who is in the world" (1 John 4:4).

6) Inocencia: a Desperate Mother

When we began preaching in the area of Cauto Cristo and opened a house church, we heard of a woman named Inocencia. She had a son who had been mentally ill since childhood. He now was a tall, strong young man who could not be controlled. He was a violent alcoholic and the situation became worse and worse. Medical science had failed to treat him; and as a last resource he was given electroshock therapy, which had caused some brain damage and seizures. As a mother, Inocencia was desperate to find help for her son, and went to a witch doctor who told her, "I have the solution." She trusted him to solve their problems, but the situation only worsened, in spite of many treatments. Inocencia was without hope, living in fear and in hellish conditions. When we invited her to come to our house church, she brought her son along. He was a constant disruption and distraction to the services, and caused considerable damage to the house.

One day I had him sit by my side on the platform and commanded him to be quiet in the name of Jesus Christ. He sat on my lap, so with one hand holding him and the other holding the Bible, I preached for about 20 minutes. Afterwards, we prayed and rebuked the sickness. At this point, we began to notice small changes in his behavior. He continued to have seizures from time to time, but they gradually began to disappear. He wandered the streets, and would awaken us every night by shouting obscenities and offensive things to us, mocking our faith. My wife and I spent many nights showing him that we loved him and wanted the best for him. We took care of him no matter how much we suffered. Inocencia was ashamed of his behavior and suffered greatly, though her faith was strengthened and she trusted that Jesus would help her son. We committed a whole day to fasting and praying for her son. After that, we experienced a great peace that made us believe that the Lord had answered our prayers. From that day forward, this young man became a living testimony of God's power and healing.

Today, Inocencia continues in her faith and is a valued sister in the church. She is grateful to God, having been transformed from a desperate mother to one who provides comfort and counsel. Never reject any person who appears to be in an impossible situation. Remember that God specializes in dealing with the impossible.

7) How Pozo Redondo Was Reached With The Gospel

We went on preaching tours every week, often accompanied by young people who were being trained as church planters. The students demonstrated the call of God on their hearts and had a strong interest in evangelism. One beautiful morning, three enthusiastic mission students, Dulce M. Almaguer, Vidalina, Marisí and Danilo Gálvez joined me on an outreach.

We began our travels very early, and after we had covered almost 13 miles arrived in the town of Tranquera. We intended to return home at the end of the day, but found that we were making slow progress as we retraced our steps after a day of preaching in Tranquera. The road conditions were very poor, and as we were without food, we felt weak and exhausted. We walked slowly in the growing darkness, aware that our safety was at risk as we travelled through unfamiliar areas in the night.

We decided to sleep outside the village of Pozo Redondo, and intended to spend the night under a tree by the road. In spite of our hunger, lack of supplies and the potential danger of being without shelter in a strange place, we trusted God for our provision. We had settled down to rest when we heard someone approaching on horseback. It was a young woman named Iliana. She was a veterinarian returning from treating a sick animal late at night. She was surprised to see us sleeping there, and as she came closer, asked us what we were doing. Once she understood that we were missionaries sharing the Gospel, she immediately took us to her home. We were allowed to bathe, have dinner and sleep in Dr. Iliana's home. We shared the gospel with Iliana and her mother, who both received Jesus as their only Savior. Some days later, Dr. Iliana donated the materials she had saved to build her house with, and a chapel was built in Pozo Redondo. Worship services were begun there, and the church continues to this day.

This tiny town experienced a new beginning as they came Jesus Christ. We came to care deeply for the very special people who were transformed by the true love of Christ. I recall a blind woman named Zoila who served us faithfully by doing all our housework and cooking our dinner each week before we went to the church. She spoke words of encouragement that helped us recover from the weariness of our long weekly journey. The children of Pozo Redondo would run to meet us as they saw the pastor and the missionaries come. Many there were changed by the Gospel's Good News.

8) The "Los Muchísimos" Gang Becomes a Church

On one side of the Cauto River was La Seis, a town with a bad reputation for having a notorious gang called "Los Muchísimos," so named because most of its members belonged to the same family. One day the Lord directed me to preach in that area. Nothing eventful happened on the first day I spent there. The people of La Seis seemed to have no interest in the Gospel. A policeman saw me and said in a mocking voice, "Pastor, we're not going to forbid you to preach here because you'll have no success in this place. They'll kick you out of here themselves!" That was not God's opinion, though. He loved the people of La Seis and the "Los Muchísimos" gang, and so they became very important to us.

Gradually, the townspeople allowed me to visit in their homes to read the Bible. A while later, a family agreed to allow us to hold a service in their home. We overflowed with joy and at the same time asked God to help us because Satan's power was well known there.

On the arranged day, we set off by bicycle to La Seis. On arriving, we realized there was an extensive power outage, and everyone had to prepare their meals outside on open fires. It grew dark and we could not see well. For a moment I did not know what to do. I went into the backyard of the meeting house, looked up to heaven and said, "Lord, what should I do? Help me!" I felt better, and when I came back into the house, I realized that many people had come to the service, but we had not seen them in the dark. My wife had begun to sing and after we prayed, we told them of God's love for them and that He was the light we all needed. I also told them about the power of God. Suddenly, a young man requested, "Pastor, pray for this sick woman who is here." I prayed and asked God to heal her. Unexpectedly, we heard people scream and the sound of a commotion in the dark. I did not know what was happening so I asked the owner of the house. "Pastor, the woman is walking! She has gotten up from her wheelchair!" Someone explained that she was 45 years old and had not been able to walk for more than eight years, and had been brought to the meeting for prayer. When we prayed she had left her wheelchair, and began to walk. We were filled with joy and we praised the Lord.

We were taken to other people to preach the Gospel. A few days later, to my surprise, Norge and his family, the leaders of the feared gang "Los Muchísimos," received Christ. They had an encounter with God's power and surrendered their lives to the service of God. They even allowed us to hold open air services in their property, which eventually became a retreat center for many churches. Later on, they built a church and parsonage with their own hands. They made musical instruments themselves, and demonstrated their love of the Lord in many ways. Their house church soon became an established church and two years later, they sent two young men to study for the pastorate at the Baptist Seminary in Santiago. Today, the church has a senior pastor and a youth pastor. They possess a deep understanding of God's power and have commissioned many missionaries and planted new churches from among their fellowship.

During the early days following the healing of the lady in the wheelchair, she joined us as we preached, proclaiming God's work in her body. Unfortunately, as she returned to a normal life, she began to drink and celebrate with friends, and failed to honor God for her healing. As a result, she became crippled again and died from cancer some time later.

The miracle God performed in that dark little house in La Seis showed that Jesus Christ was powerful and zealous for those He has called to Himself. The frightening and hardened "Los Muchísimos" gang of La Seis turned out to be the foundation of a dynamic missionary church. Go in obedience wherever God sends you to, because Jesus can turn the worst of men and situations into an inspiration for many.

9) We Have No Food

I clearly remember an October afternoon in the tiny town of Babiney. I had left home early on a bicycle to get to a mission site that was 6 miles away. It was a long day of hard work and many hours in the heat. As I returned home about 4:00pm, the sun was still blazing down on me. When I arrived home, I felt exhausted. I greeted my family, anxious for something to eat. My wife replied anxiously, "we have no food." As I lowered myself into a wooden chair, I thought, "I don't have any money, or any place to go to get food, but I believe that God won't let us go hungry." In that faith, I prayed with my family for food that afternoon and told my wife, "Turn on the stove and fill a pot with some water." Soledad placed the water to boil while I took a shower, and then played with my kids on their bed.

About 40 minutes had passed when Soledad told me that the water in the pot was boiling away. I went to another room and prayed, "Lord, you know all things. We have worked hard and we are hungry. My family needs food; please perform a miracle. God, have mercy on us. Amen."

I remained sitting on the floor when I finished my prayer, my head leaned against the bed. I heard someone knock on the door. When I opened it, a man I didn't know asked me, "Does the Pastor live here?" "Yes, I'm the pastor," I answered. He handed me a package and told me, "I was at home butchering a pig when I heard a voice that said to me, 'Take some pork to the pastor. Take some pork to the pastor.' So the voice would stop bothering me, I asked around to find out where you lived."

My wife and I thanked the Lord, looked at each other, and praised God for His mercies. We hurried off to the kitchen to start cooking. A little while later, Sister Celeste showed up with some sweet potatoes and Brother Gabriel gave us some of his rice. We ate very well that day because of God's miracle. God is still providing His manna today. He is the same yesterday, today, and forever.

The Bible is right when it says: "Look at the birds of the air, for they neither sow nor reap nor gather into barns; yet your heavenly Father feeds them. Are you not of more value than they?" Matthew 6:26. These experiences made us depend on God more and more. We learned to wait on Him and believe that He who called us won't forsake us. The Lord has enough resources to do His work and take care of us.

10) Two Different Women, Two Different Ways

Martha and Elena were sisters. They felt their need for the Lord so much that they sought to discover more of Him. They frequently came to our services, travelling three miles on foot to get to the meetings, and showed great interest in the Lord. When their husbands found out that they were coming to church they became very angry. These sisters risked being beaten for their new beliefs. I advised them that they should love their husbands, but not give up their faith.

One day their husbands said, "You are going to have to choose, it's either God or us". Martha remained quiet, and sought to love her husband every day. Once she was sewing a shirt in her living room while she sang:

My God is everywhere.
My God is everywhere.
My God is everywhere.
Praise the Lord.

If you look for Him in the mountains,
If you look for Him in the sea,
If you look for Him in heaven,
You'll find Him there.

Her husband Peter overheard her song, and became furious. "If I don't leave right now, I'll beat you to death," and he dashed out of the house and went to a nearby store. As he neared the counter, he started humming, "My God is everywhere, My God is everywhere." The salesman asked, "Hey, Peter, what's that tune you're singing?" When he realized he was singing his wife's song, he again became very angry. I believe the Spirit did a great work in Peter's heart right there.

When this happened, he went back home at once, took a bath and dressed up as if he was going to a special place. Martha, who was not aware that anything had happened, got dinner ready for him, and tiptoed out to church. When she returned from church, she found Peter sitting in the living room, all dressed up, just as she had left him. "What's wrong?" she asked timidly. He answered, "If you had invited me to come to church, I would have joined you." She stood in awe, not knowing what to do. It was then that he told her about the experience he had, of how he hummed a church chorus unconsciously. From that day on, he proved himself faithful to the Lord. He later became a deacon, serving the church faithfully.

Elena, the other sister, had said to her husband, "If I had to choose between God and you, I choose you and to hell with the church." Soon after that, her husband, an alcoholic, tried to kill her. Her house had become a living hell, and sadly, a few days later, she committed suicide, leaving two small children to the care of her husband.

It's been impossible for me to forget this story. This is a vivid example about decision making. It teaches that the result of following Christ brings life, and to follow Satan results in death.

11) The Outcasts Become Glorious

When we started pastoring in Babiney, we encountered many disabled people. Among these unfortunate people were children and adults who were both blind and deaf. Their extreme disability prevented them from being involved in normal activities or relationships. They were rejected by the community and their preferences, needs, and decisions were often ignored. Some were ridiculed and forced to drink alcohol until they became drunk, and then mocked in public. Three

Group of deaf mutes performing a drama of the crucifixion.

of these people attended our church regularly, but were often ignored and left the services never knowing what had been preached.

God touched our hearts and showed us that He could change the lives of those with deaf/dumb disabilities. My wife helped me start a Sunday school in our living room. We began with eight students and we learned to communicate with them, teaching them through a special code using touch and sign language. They were able to learn the Bible easily.

It was impossible for many to understand how these brothers with disabilities could grasp the concepts taught in Bible classes, and to practice what they had learned. Each Sunday, visitors who came to the church were greatly moved by the experience of worshipping along side the deaf/dumb portion of the congregation.

God began to glorify Himself and bless the ministry of these new believers. Our spare-time activity of learning sign language began to reap a harvest within the church. Some of these new believers discovered that they could make people laugh through acting, some were able to create pleasing art using newly discovered artistic talents. Others were given a ministry of intersession for the sick, and God often miraculously answered their fervent prayers. They became collaborators in many aspects of our ministry. In 1990, we founded a ministry called Speaking Hands, inspired by those disabled brothers who displayed God's glory.

As the reputation of these faithful brothers grew, they began to receive many visitors from all over the country, including the national presidents of the National Association for Deaf People and the National Association for Blind People. We were also invited to a World Congress in Argentina, where members of Speaking Hands were awarded various prizes for their accomplishments and handicraft exhibits. The fruit of this ministry has given new life to many disabled individuals, as well as providing inspiration to others. Feature articles in national magazines and newspapers have spread the message of God's care for the disabled throughout Cuba, impacting a changing attitude regarding the value of the disabled.

Many interpreters were trained to help the disabled understand the preaching at church, and to communicate better in their daily lives. Today, workshops and classes continue where those with disabilities are able to learn work skills and be actively involved in ministry and social events.

The success of the Speaking Hands ministry was accomplished through hard work, and though we were often criticized by others, we enjoyed helping build Christ's character in these dear brothers and sisters. They are now respected by those who once taunted them. Our time and investment with them taught us to value human life as God does and to see how God's grace fell marvelously upon these people.

12) Bernardo Can't Read

I'd like to talk about an ordinary man who God used to do extraordinary things. He lives in Limoncito, an isolated village populated by people of Haitian descent. Set in a sea of sugarcane, where heavy dust from the dirt roads makes it difficult to breathe, the village consists of a tractor repair shop, some farm machinery and a sugar cane mill. A boy named Bernardo Martinez grew up there. He started school when he was six, but would sneak out of school at every opportunity to hide in the sugarcane, where he was never caught by the teachers. Although he was forced to attend the classes, he was never was able to learn. Bernardo started school when he was 6 and on his 14th birthday was still in the first grade.

Bernardo was finally transferred to a school for mentally retarded children for a year, but he left that school still unable to learn. He could not read, and was unable to even identify vowels from consonants. Everyone gave up on him, and there seemed no hope for him. His mother forced him to work tilling the land. Eventually, he taught himself to play percussion instruments and became part of local amateur street bands playing Cuban and Haitian folk dance music. He began to go to parties as a musician, where the dances often ended in unruly fighting among the partiers.

I met Bernardo on one of my evangelistic trips. God sent me to Limoncito where I met Rebecca, a young woman who had recently received Christ through the witness of her father, Lefrán, a Haitian believer. Lefrán had been praying for the salvation of his family and the community for many years, and had a burden for the people of his Haitian homeland. Rebecca told me that she was living with a man although they were not married. The man was Bernardo. We began to pray for him. This first visit was the beginning of a new church in Limoncito.

As the young church grew, many people shared the Gospel with Bernardo, but his answer was always the same, "I don't understand anything." One night we showed the Jesus film. Bernardo wept and was touched by the Holy Spirit, but made no personal decision. A few days later, as he attended a fellowship meeting where many people from different churches were meeting, and he publicly received Christ in his heart. The time of prayer lasted nearly four hours, and Bernardo prayed on his knees in a corner of the church.

After the prayer time he could not get up on his feet so I helped him stand. As he stood, I was impressed with the sense that God would use him mightily. I embraced him saying, "You and I are brothers now." "Am I becoming a Christian now?" he asked. As his understanding grew, Bernardo became secure in his commitment and stand for Christ. Bernardo was among the first class who attended the Church Planter Training School in 1991, when the Youth With a Purpose ministry was just beginning.

When Bernardo began at the Church Planter Training School, everything appeared to be going well, but one day I saw him sobbing uncontrollably in the church. I approached him but he would tell me nothing. His wife motioned to me, and quietly said, "He's been suffering greatly since his conversion, because he is unable to read." I was surprised because illiteracy in Cuba is very rare. I approached him and gave him a hug. "God is going to help you and you'll be able to read the Bible." God opened his ability to read, and today Bernardo is a graduate trained by the Youth With a Purpose Bible and Missions Seminary and works as the pastor in Limoncito.

Pastor Bernardo was used by God to bless our family during the difficult days of the Special Period. Sometimes, when we had nothing to eat, he would arrive at our home, having made the 22 mile round trip either on foot or bicycle. He sacrificially gave us food, sometimes saving his own portion to share with us. His faithfulness led us to a very close friendship. He became my personal advisor and wise counsellor. He founded and still directs the fine musical group called Worshipers of the King, and founded the Intercession Team that has been faithfully praying for us since 1991. His prayers are answered today, and he is acknowledged as a great man of faith. Many families are grateful to him for his love towards the lost, and count him as their spiritual father. He has an open heart for missions and evangelism. This once ordinary, rejected, and illiterate man has become a useful and valued instrument in God's hands.

13) A Month With No Salary

A group of missionary families were preparing to plant new churches. Their salaries and ministry costs were dependant on offerings from the local churches. These families had given up everything to serve the Lord. One day, our account had no more money and we did not know what to do to meet these needs. The situation was very difficult. We sought the Lord, believing that He would open the door of provision on their behalf.

My wife suggested that we sell the living room furniture we had just bought. I stared at her anxiously, knowing that she had prayed for many years for these items. It seemed an unreasonable thing to do, but I realized she was freely willing to give up something she really loved. I told her I agreed, aware of the sacrifice that she was making. We found that we could get only $ 260 US dollars for the items by selling them so quickly, but we urgently needed to pay the missionaries. We made arrangements, and a buyer said he would come the following morning.

After making these plans, we heard a car stop outside our house, and then someone knocked on the door. The man who introduced himself was a pastor from Havana. He said,

"As I was driving past your town, God led me to come this way, say hello and pray for you." We prayed together, and though we did not know him, we were blessed by his visit, and God used his prayers on our behalf. Shortly after he left, and while we were still talking of the unexpected visit, he returned, accompanied by another man who was visiting from overseas. The pastor explained that the foreign brother had felt led to give us an envelope, and so they had returned. Then they said a quick "God bless you!" to us and left. We tore the envelope open and found $300 dollars. What a surprise! That was exactly what we needed for our missionaries.

My wife and I hugged each other and praised God. We did not have to sell our furniture; the Lord wanted to bless us. The Lord has faithfully provided this support monthly ever since. He is the One who supports Youth With a Purpose and the other ministries of The Redeemer Baptist Church. We are committed to the work of the Lord, and He will always bless and provide for His own.

14) "Your Son Will Die. We Did All We Could."

In August 1997, I attended a Latin American Youth Congress in Mexico where I had been invited to speak. I returned to Cuba rejoicing in the success of the conference, and anticipating the reunion with my family. At the airport, I was welcomed home by Carlitos, who was 11, and Liannette, 7, who were excitedly waiting by their mother's side. The three of them ran to meet me, and we hugged and kissed affectionately as Cubans do. I treasure the memories of that reunion, and the blessings of my family. We traveled to my parent's home in Jatibonico, where we stayed a few hours. In Mexico I had obtained special gifts for the family, and Carlitos was delighted with an outfit of new clothing which he immediately put on, declaring that they were "really cool."

While I had been at the conference, my wife had directed our move from Babiney, helped by our church family, to Céspedes, where we had taken a new pastorate. After visiting our family, we left for Céspedes with my cousin, Leandro, who drove us to our new home in his car. He was driving back to Jatibonico the same evening, and it had been arranged for Carlitos to ride with him.

Our new congregation was looking forward to our arrival, and when we entered the Céspedes church for the first time, I felt joy and anticipation in continuing God's work there and becoming their pastor! As I was meeting some of the brothers, my wife suddenly burst into the room and said in great desperation, "There's been an accident!"

My cousin's car had hit a tractor as they drove to Jatibonico. The front windshield had shattered on impact and Carlitos had been badly injured by the flying glass. He suffered extensive cuts to his face, including lacerations to his jugular and carotid vessels and eye. He was alive, but in shock when I arrived at the small hospital in the town of Florida. I was told he had no chance for survival. My heart shrank, I wept and experienced intense pain like no other I have ever felt. I raced to the surgery suite where I could see Carlitos' blood-stained clothes that he had worn for the first time that day, lying on the floor. Dr. Cedeño, a member of our church, came and told me, "I'm so sorry; we did all we could." She later explained that it had taken 30 minutes to transfer Carlitos from the accident scene to the hospital. Both vessels that carry blood to the brain had been damaged, much blood had been lost, and his circulation compromised. Both brain and vital organ damage had occurred from the lack of oxygen during this time. In spite of blood transfusions and every treatment available, there was no hope. Dr. Cedeño suffered as she broke the news to me.

Some pastors and Christian brothers who had gathered tried to comfort me. Many said, "Your son is going to die."

His mother was being taken care of at home while the final arrangements were being made to receive the corpse. In her grief she could not cry, but had severe cramps in her arms and legs and became faint. In her grief, she pictured the funeral; our son in a coffin as it was carried into the service. Many people were crying yet she was unable to gather the strength to even go inside. As this scene unfolded in her mind, she realized it was an attack from Satan.

Unexpectedly, Soledad remembered a picture we had given our son as a present. It portrayed a boy with a baseball bat, ball, and glove sitting thoughtfully on a rock. Below this image was an inscription that read, "*Everything* is possible with God's help." Instantly, the terrible cramping began to resolve, and an inner strength drove her to prayer, where with all her faith she cried out before the Lord. "Lord, I believe that You are raising my son from the dead right now. The devil wants to destroy us, but he knows he can't make us give up our vision and calling in this place. He won't succeed. We're not afraid because we know in whom we have believed. Satan, though we will suffer at the loss of our son, we are persuaded that he's in heaven with Christ and this gives us the strength and confidence to carry on."

My wife was strengthened, but she felt that her heart was breaking. Our daughter cried for her brother, not really understanding what had occurred. Many Christian friends and pastors like Rev. Obed Morales and his family provided comfort to us, and helped us withstand in faith.

When I was able to see my son, his lifeless body was pale, his face and eye bandaged. Our friends were there and the doctor stood close by, sadly shaking his head as if to say, "Nothing else could have been done." I felt my heart would burst as I came near my son. I ran my hand over his bandaged wounds and kissed him goodbye.

Suddenly, I heard God's voice clearly speak to me in the crowded room. "My son, you and I have a covenant with this child." Immediately, I remembered my wife's pregnancy when specialists had informed us that Carlitos would likely be born with a hydrocephalic malformation, a missing organ; or would suffer from sickle-cell anemia. We were strongly urged to terminate the pregnancy. We went to our church to pray and await God's answer to this dilemma. After we had been on our knees some time, I sensed God's peace and the certainty that He was against the termination. We accepted this in faith and told the doctor that we believed we were to carry the pregnancy to term and trust God for the results.

When my wife gave birth, Carlitos had no disease or malformation. We went to see the specialist, and when he saw the baby he said in great amazement, "This can't be the right child; they must have brought me the wrong medical history." We told him that our son was the same child he had been treating, and that God had performed a miracle.

I had prayed from the time of Carlitos' birth that God would make him His servant. My prayer had been, "Lord, if he is not going to be a true Christian, I'd rather you took him to Your presence before he turns five." This may sound odd to many, but I meant it with all my heart. I remember that on December 1, 1991, Carlitos' fifth birthday, I was in Bible school over 300 miles away from him. That evening I walked along the riverbank anticipating God's answer and prayed till midnight. I called home the following morning and Soledad told me that Carlitos was fine. I was then assured that God had answered, having made a covenant with me for Carlitos.

I thought of that covenant during the trying period I was going through. As my son's body lay before me, I trusted the voice of God, and laid my hands on his cold little body, praying loudly as the Spirit inspired me before the Heavenly Father.

Suddenly, someone screamed, "The child is moving, he's breathing!" Immediately, the doctors set to work to assist his breathing, because his lungs had been damaged as well. Carlitos was urgently transferred to the main hospital in

Camagüey, where advanced life support facilities were available.

There was no room for me in the ambulance and I was asked, "What are you going to do? Are you alright?" I simply replied, "It's alright. The child will not die." We had to wait only a few days to see God's answer. After only two weeks, Carlitos was released from the hospital safe and sound. Joyfully, we held a service to thank God for this miracle.

Later, eight doctors and some nurses traveled to Céspedes and spoke to the 800 people who attended the service of thanksgiving. Carlitos preached a message entitled *We Need To Be Ready* and many people came to know the Lord.

Today, Carlitos serves the Lord working for Youth With a Purpose, as the design editor and computer specialist. He also plays the bass guitar for the Worshippers of the King music ministry. He has participated in several evangelistic concerts and crusades held throughout Cuba. He completed studies at the Youth With a Purpose Seminary on January 30th 2005, receiving a Bachelor's of Theology degree.

"I know that whatever God does, it shall be forever. Nothing can be added to it, and nothing taken from it. God does it, that men should fear before Him. That which is has already been, and what is to be has already been; And God requires an account of what is past." Ecclesiastes 3: 14-15

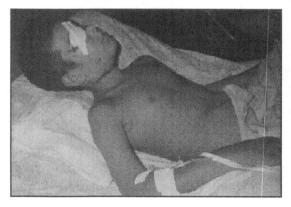

Carlitos, days after the terrible car accident.

15) A Missionary Trip To Haiti

Lefrán, our Haitian brother of steadfast faith from Limoncito, who gave his home to be used as the church, had a vision for bringing the Gospel to Haiti. He frequently encouraged me to visit his native land to preach the Gospel. I had prayed for five years to be allowed to go, without an opening. In the summer of 1999, I did receive a visa to visit the United States, and the arrangements were made for me to travel. As I was preparing to leave, something happened that I did not expect. My plans changed at the last moment when I heard the audible voice of Christ say, "Go to Haiti." Although there was a strong desire in my heart to preach in Haiti, I was also very excited about the trip to the U.S., as I believed that this trip would be a source of greater support for the ministry. I was suddenly forced to choose between my plans and what appeared to be God's leading. I must admit that initially, I could not believe what was happening. To me, it seemed unreasonable and impossible, but I knew that God's thoughts were often different from mine. After a few anxious minutes of deliberation, I made the best decision: to obey.

I immediately went to the Haitian Embassy in Havana. It was Wednesday and I had no Haitian visa. An airplane would leave Cuba for Haiti on Thursday morning. I had less than 24 hours to get the visa, the plane ticket, a bus ticket and to travel from Havana to Santiago de Cuba. It would be impossible by human standards to make the 560 mile trip to Santiago in time, but this very impossibility motivated me to move forward, trusting God. I said to myself, "This is quite difficult for me, but if it's of God, everything will fall into place." I was confident that He would lead my steps.

When I got to the embassy, the consul said he could not give me the visa in time, and that it would cost a great deal if I were to request it immediately. The consul turned away and I had no chance to explain myself. I went to the secretary and asked her to help me; saying, "God has called me to Haiti." She grinned as if to say, "He's nuts!" I begged her, "Please, hand my passport to him and tell him that God sent me." She was reluctant to do it, but finally agreed, perhaps just to get rid of me. She took my passport and disappeared into the offices. Half an hour of precious travel time dragged by.

She finally reappeared, and with a smile asked, "Who are you?" I answered, "Why do you ask?" She held out my passport, shaking her head and said: "You've been granted a visa for Haiti." It was about 1.00 pm, and I quickly headed for the travel agency to buy the plane ticket. There was a ticket available, and after I paid for it said, "I have a problem. I don't have time to get to Santiago by bus before the flight leaves." They directed me to a domestic flights agent, who informed me that there were no flights scheduled from Havana to Santiago that day

I bowed my head in great disappointment and decided to leave, not knowing what else to do. As I walked out of the travel agency, a phone rang and the domestic agent called out to me, "Sir, sir! I've just been informed that the plane for Haiti broke down and that the flight has now been re-routed to begin here in Havana." She said smiling, "You're a lucky guy. I'll give you a ticket to Santiago and you will be able to go on to Haiti on the same flight." She did not understand that it was God, not luck, who had created a way in the midst of the impossible to allow this trip.

When I arrived at the Port-au-Prince, Haiti Airport, I did not know what to do. I knew no one, and had only one contact's address that had been given to me in Cuba. I had only enough money for the airport tax and 30 dollars to last throughout the whole trip. And I spoke no French.

As I was considering what to do, a taxi driver who spoke a little Spanish approached me and asked "Where do you want to go?" I handed him the address and explained that I was a Cuban pastor on a mission trip in Haiti. He told me, "I drive for the pastor of my church." I smiled and said as I shook my head, "Lord, you're awesome!" He took me to my contact, a family who shared their food with me.

We went for a walk together, and took advantage of the time to pray for the city. I was later invited to visit the port city of Aux Cayes. We traveled through the mountains on a big truck where I was able to present the gospel to a young Spanish- speaking man who received Christ. He was a student who studied in the Doninican Replubic, and became a great blessing while I was there, serving as a translator. This gave me the opportunity to share the Gospel with street children in Aux Cayes. The children on the streets would tell me, "Feed me first and then tell me about God."

I began to make friends and win the trust of people gradually. I also had the privilege of preaching in a fellowship where several churches had gathered. I was able to visit other churches as well. Sometimes, I slept on porches of homes or had nothing to eat, and one time I was mugged, but God took care of me.

God granted me some significant experiences. The mayor of Aux Cayes fell sick and a Cuban doctor who was working there invited me to go with him to visit the mayor. The mayor's mother-in-law was Cuban-born and could speak some Spanish. I shared God's love with the family and prayed for the mayor and his family. They hosted us for a

With the family in Haiti that hosted me.

delicious meal afterwards. I also visited an orphanage and was able to pave the way for other missionaries be sent to this country.

I am thankful for the missionary experience and exposure I had in Haiti, and feel a bond with these people. I am particularly thankful for the friends who hosted me there. God never forsook me and has given me a vision and desire to return in the future to minister to them.

We are currently training and preparing missionaries and pastors to be sent out to Haiti, particularly those of Haitian descent. When the time is ripe, we will go to Haiti as missionaries. Three Haitian brothers are currently studying in our seminary, preparing to preach the Gospel, to plant churches and to share in the same vision that Brother Lefrán has for spreading the Gospel from Cuba to Haiti.

5

An Important Decision

It is a wonderful thing and an awesome responsibility to be able to hear the voice of God, His word, and to know His plans and His purposes. When we think of this, we are tempted to say to God, "I'm not ready." At these times God insists, because He knows what He wants and wishes to accomplish through us. The Lord Jesus Christ says, in case of doubt, "If I have called you, I'll take care of you. Take courage, don't doubt. Whether you go through the valley or the mountain, I'll go with you."

When we accept God's call, others may not understand us. Carrying out a mission brings about great struggles. We face diverse situations that we don't understand. We feel we are obeying God, and yet, everything appears to grow more difficult. People we believe are there to help us suddenly withdraw their support, and times come when we feel very alone. It is then that we feel as though we were in Gethsemane. At these times, God sends an angel there to strengthen us. Even if our isolation leaves us feeling at a stagnant end, a peaceful wind of God's assurance will bring us peace. Suddenly, we can hear Jesus say, "You are my Son, today I have begotten You. Ask of Me and I will give you the nations for your inheritance and the ends of the earth for your possession" (Psalms 2: 7-8).

Our missionary ministry called Youth With a Purpose: Cuba for Christ and the Nations faced a season of attack. Some people lied about us. Some leaders would not agree that we were responding to God's call, and believed that His work should be performed only through the churches. Satan was trying to deceive them; and caused their attacks to be targeted against all aspects of our ministry.

This situation hurt us deeply, but we fought in our defense. There was a time when we even doubted if we were doing God's will. Many things caused us to suffer, especially when those who had once been fellow workers and friends of the ministry; "our people"— the ones we loved, trusted, and whose advice, protection and understanding we had always relied on — began to oppose and criticize us openly. It was then that we realized that we could either retreat, locking ourselves in our own ivory tower, or we could "go up to Gethsemane."

The many sufferings and trials I had to go through helped me see a marvelous God who defends what He wants because He is sovereign. During four years of loneliness and rejection, the most valuable achievements of my life were accomplished. I learned to walk with Christ in a very special way. During that time, God raised a team of men and women dedicated to working out the mission that He had called us to. We determined to work tirelessly so that His call would be fulfilled in us. Through the years, we have been able to see that God supports and accomplishes the purpose to which He has called us.

I was once asked back then, "Why don't you promote yourself?" I answered, "I want God to be made known through what we do, not for me to be lifted up." We are useless servants in our own power. What we do by His grace alone will be manifested in due time.

Once we moved out of the tower of defensiveness and isolation, we realized that the time for fulfilling His call had actually come. People began to look at us differently. They would greet us with a smile. Men of vision started to be raised up from diverse nationalities and races. Leaders today truly understand the real purpose of our ministry: a visionary generation committed to the belief that "now is the time."

We are called to serve God by partnering with local churches, cooperating with God's steady and comprehensive work throughout Cuba and to all nations. We believe that each ministry is a valuable tool that He will use for His glory. Ministries are not to compete among themselves, but to join together to please Him who has called them. This unity is a symbol of our Savior's plan for His people and of His Church. Men are not to tell God what to do; it is God who determines what will be done and how it is going to be accomplished.

If we faithfully endure suffering, misunderstanding, mockery and attempts to steal God's vision from us, we will begin to see fruit develop with the passing of time. We will learn that God intends to teach us to be consecrated to the vision and mission He has called us to carry out. I am thankful for the experiences of difficulty we endured. They looked like defeats at first, yet they have taught me to walk with my hand in the Lord's, and to depend only on Him. I have learned how important it is to be faithful to my call. I better understand what dealing with God Almighty is like; that He exists by His own power, He does not depend on anyone to exist or succeed, and that He is sovereign and deserves our respect, worship and praise.

If you are in the right place, doing God's will but in spite of this you feel lonely and discouraged, remember that times of difficulty are a good opportunity for you to train yourself to walk with Him. You will become prepared and equipped for what He has in His will for you. He has allowed these times and uses them to shape us into His Son's character.

During this process, He will release those who are a burden to you, those without spiritual eyes, who are focused on earthly things and who fail to see the dimension and depth of His majesty. He will rid you of those who are conformed to the triviality offered by this world. He will send others who will provide help and support, so that working together you might accomplish your mission and call.

The apostle Paul knew about suffering, both physical and emotional. He understood difficulties and trials. Yet he remained faithful to Christ and to the Gospel. So, as an encouragement I'd like you to read Paul's words in Galatians 1:11 to 2:10:

> But I make known to you, brethren, that the gospel which was preached by me is not according to man. For I neither received it from man, nor was I taught it, but it came through the revelation of Jesus Christ.
>
> For you have heard of my former conduct in Judaism, how I persecuted the church of God beyond measure and tried to destroy it. And I advanced in Judaism beyond many of my contemporaries in my own nation, being more exceedingly zealous for the traditions of my fathers.
>
> But when it pleased God, who separated me from my mother's womb and called me through His grace, to reveal His Son in me, that I might preach Him among the Gentiles, I did not immediately confer with flesh and blood, nor did I go up to Jerusalem to those who were apostles before me; but I went to Arabia, and returned again to Damascus. Then after three years I went up to Jerusalem to see Peter, and remained with him fifteen days. But I saw none of the other apostles except James, the Lord's brother. (Now concerning the things which I write to you, indeed, before God, I do not lie.)

Afterward I went into the regions of Syria and Cilicia. And I was unknown by face to the churches of Judea which were in Christ. But they were hearing only, "He who formerly persecuted us now preaches the faith which he once tried to destroy." And they glorified God in me.

Then after fourteen years I went up again to Jerusalem with Barnabas, and also took Titus with me. And I went up by revelation, and communicated to them that gospel which I preach among the Gentiles, but privately to those who were of reputation, lest by any means I might run, or had run, in vain. Yet not even Titus who was with me, being a Greek, was compelled to be circumcised.

And this occurred because of false brethren secretly brought in (who came in by stealth to spy out our liberty which we have in Christ Jesus, that they might bring us into bondage), to whom we did not yield submission even for an hour, that the truth of the gospel might continue with you.

But from those who seemed to be something—whatever they were, it makes no difference to me; God shows personal favoritism to no man—for those who seemed to be something added nothing to me.

But on the contrary, when they saw that the gospel for the uncircumcised had been committed to me, as the gospel for the circumcised was to Peter (for He who worked effectively in Peter for the apostleship to the circumcised also worked effectively in me toward the Gentiles), and when James, Cephas, and John, who seemed to be pillars, perceived the grace that had been given to me, they gave me and Barnabas the right hand of fellowship, that we should go to the Gentiles and they to the circumcised.

They desired only that we should remember the poor, the very thing which I also was eager to do.

Whenever God has a plan, He prepares His children for the work they will be sent to do. Obeying Him is so important that it becomes necessary to diligently bear the Cross, and be refined in the furnace. We are grateful to the Lord for leading each step and every decision we have taken throughout the years of intense labor.

6

Starting the Bible School

From the very beginning of the ministry, we met together to design strategies and to study the Bible. Our vision for evangelism was received so strongly in our church that children, young people, and adults actively joined in the work of planting new missions and home churches, and in carrying out evangelistic activities. We walked for many miles, but because we had the Great Commission in our hearts, we did not grow weary with the hardship. We founded four churches and twelve missions in three years, but found that there were too few of us to provide the proper support that the new works deserved, and so we redirected our attention from beginning new programs to training new workers who could provide support to new communities of believers.

Although we had a vision, we did not know how to go about establishing a school. We had neither the place nor the money for a school, so we started to pray and the Lord began to lead our steps. Early in 1992, it became clear that we shouldn't wait for all the recourses to become available before taking the first steps. What we did have was enough. We possessed vision, the will to work, and the young people willing to take on the task. The shade of a luxurious tree in one of our church sister's back yard became a classroom, the tree's roots became the chairs, and without giving it a second thought, the Church Planting School was started.

Adolescents, young adults, and new converts who had a heart for missions attended the classes with great interest and dedication. The drive and devotion that characterized the students of the school was extraordinary. Traveling long distances, the lack of transportation, a frequent lack of food and books, and the hot sun were all obstacles that could have slowed the willingness of the students, but nothing put out the fire they had for missions..

As I returned home from teaching in those early days, I wept and said to God, "We have no paper, pencils, blackboards, or textbooks for them." We had only my Bible and a commentary on Matthew. My wife comforted me, encouraging me to persevere, bearing in mind God's call to train a generation of young men and women with a purpose. Every time I thought of this, my faith was strengthened. I knew that Jesus was the owner of the vision and that He would also be our provision.

A few days after we began classes, some brothers gave us used paper with one blank side. Although some of the pages were very old, it allowed the students to take notes from the lectures and increased the process of learning. Once the daily lectures began, we often lost track of time. We were happy in the Lord for what was being accomplished.

A wonderful thing happened one day as my wife returned from an evangelistic trip. She carried a box with her and handed it to me as a gift. I was amazed to find a small typewriter in the box. I jumped for joy and asked her, "How did you buy it? How much did it cost?" She told me, "It doesn't matter; now you have something to write your lectures with." I later learned that it had cost 1000 pesos; a large sum of money. She had probably sold something of great value to get it. Soledad understood how important it was to the school. We then were able type our lessons, lectures and tests.

More students came to the school, and it grew to a class of 30. The secretarial work increased, and we found volunteers who spent many hours typing lecture notes and tests for the students. Five years of intense work passed. Our crusades and rallies became more effective and we trained workers in each of the mission sites. Out of the 30 original church planters trained that first year, 28 are still actively working for the

Lord as pastors and missionaries. Others are leaders in the Youth With a Purpose ministry.

To earn money, we cut wood, charred it in kilns and made some charcoal to sell. We used that money to support our outreach activities and to support missionaries. I cannot remember that any of these men or women ever complained about the difficulties they regularly faced. They were convinced of their call.

When God took us to Céspedes in 1997, He blessed us with a congregation who had a heart for the work of Youth With a Purpose ministry and seminary. A time of blessing and answers to our prayers began as these faithful partners joined with us. The Lord allowed us to work with very special people, who had a love for His work. The names of many of these saints are written both on our hearts and in the Book of Life, as some of them have passed away.

In 1998, some foreign brothers blessed us greatly when they gave us an electric typewriter as a present. This was awesome because we were able to produce much clearer work more quickly. These men of God also offered to help us with a Bible training course for pastors. New church planters registered in this study program and this is how the Youth with a Purpose Theological Seminary began. This program had great success, and many pastors and churches wrote saying that they wanted to train their leaders as well. We realized then, that more training programs were urgently needed to meet this need, to increase the potential of the Church as well as the effectiveness of leaders so as to reach more people with the Gospel.

Our ministry board agreed to create a department for training programs. A principal and secretary were selected, who worked in partnership with the School Board. Their charge was to supervise the theological training and education aspects of the ministry. We had many days of hard work, and carefully set goals that reflected the original vision of advancing the Gospel in Cuba and to the nations.

These were the agreements:

1) Replace the former *School for Church Planters* with a *Theological Missionary Seminary*.
2) Keep and reinforce the on-site courses and classes.
3) Prepare a curriculum based on books written by our own teachers that would help students gain a broader theological knowledge using fewer required texts. This curriculum was called the *Extension Course*. This opened new doors for us to create schools in every church with their own trained teacher staff.

In our first two programs, 132 students from across Cuba registered, from Guantánamo to Santi Espíritu. I had the electric typewriter, an old computer and a printer, so I started to publish the first text. We often prayed, "Lord, don't let this printer break down!" We would spend the whole day printing out study materials for the student body across Cuba. The printer usually overheated, but God always took care of it.

We began to see amazing results from the Bible classes, and our churches experienced great evangelistic growth. There was a real need for assistant pastors, youth pastors, children's pastors and missionaries in the church communities who had specific training and the heart of a pastor. That's how we helped the Church grow and allowed pastors to pray and study the Word of God more effectively and with greater focus.

Typically, churches expected only one pastor who was supposed to be a "jack of all trades" and do it all. Actually, most pastors were neglecting their spiritual life and Bible study to take care of the congregation. No wonder many have been snared by sin. We need to get closer to God to be better leaders. Desiring to assist pastors and local churches, we started a third curriculum called the *Regular Course*. This training focuses on three main areas: highly qualified professors, a quality curriculum, and an exhaustive library. This curriculum has now been successfully implemented.

Our miracle-working God has allowed us to live wonderful times. He always keeps His promises. He has used godly people who provided resources faithfully. We now have 17 professors, who all have degrees in Biblical Studies, and many of them are taking master's level courses through the B. H. Carroll Theological Institute.

With 1,200 students from 40 different denominations now enrolled, we face new challenges. But our goal is still to reach the world with the knowledge of God.

We thank our King that what He began in 1991 has come true. Cuba and the world are being reached through theological and Biblical education, and the work expands yearly. Glory to God!

Our school started underneath a large tree!

7

Evangelistic Crusades from East to West

We have had the vision to hold evangelistic crusades since 1991. Passion for the lost grew in our hearts over time. My love for Cuba is very strong. God allowed me to be born in this nation, and it was here that I met the most precious one in the world: Jesus Christ, my Savior. I started dreaming of preaching all across the nation, but I did not know how to do it. We prayed to the Lord daily, seeking His will and wisdom. Whenever I told people about the fire within me to reach out to the whole of Cuba, they did not support me or believe it could be done. They believed that working within the local church was enough. They would remind me that I had no resources and that the county was facing very difficult times, and it would not be good to get involved. I thought differently, though. My heart was filled with passion and fervent desire to carry out this vision.

One day, my wife realized my frustration and told me, "If you feel God is leading you, just get started. He'll help you because He's called you." I talked to some young people and they said, "Pastor, we believe all you're saying, we want to join you." I was encouraged, so we began to take the first steps gradually. We invited some Christian youth to visit places where no church had ever been planted to preach the Gospel. The first converts from that evangelism trip encouraged us. We initiated home-based small groups for these new believers to fellowship in. They were from 3 to 18 miles away from one another. We visited these groups weekly, sometimes on foot, and sometimes by bicycle. We sometimes had to go on horseback and stay overnight. Winning a soul to

Christ had become an ardent passion burning in the heart of every child, youngster and adult in our church.

I stood under the starry sky one night, looked up and said to the Lord, "I'd like to have evangelistic crusades all across Cuba, help me!" Peace enveloped my heart and I could feel His support. I learned to depend on and trust His Word. My vision implied demands and needs that no man could have ever met individually, so I had to trust God Almighty.

I studied Paul's missionary journeys, as well as Jesus' commissioning of the twelve disciples, followed by the seventy. I saw that whoever He sent He empowered with authority and ability to spread His kingdom on the Earth. I became so excited that I could not keep this truth to myself, and I told many pastors about it. However, they did not understand why one would walk through a whole town handing out tracts and Bibles. Many believed that Bibles should be only for Christians because they feared that most people who received Bibles might not come back to church, and the books would be lost. Others feared that such activity could cause political or social trouble.

When I shared with them the idea of churches joining together for a mass crusade or evangelism activity, they did not accept this either. Many pastors would not associate with one another. Some churches would not welcome brothers from other denominations to the crusades. They also would not tolerate the idea of receiving people with long hair or earrings, improperly-dressed women, prostitutes, homosexuals or other "undesirables" in our churches. During this period of the early 1990's, many churches in Cuba misused the idea of having a "holy zeal for God's house" to protect themselves from the discomfort of dealing with the unchurched. How we have struggled to change that mentality!

We insisted that it did not matter how people came, but that we were to love and reach out to all those who need Christ. Only Jesus could transform them, not us. We learned by experience that many young people with tattoos and extravagant clothes who received Christ after attending the crusades became awesome leaders in our meetings, loving the lost. They helped unsaved people avoid the suffering and emptiness they had experienced in their past.

Ready for an evangelistic trip.

Problems and negative responses from others often discouraged me. It seemed I would never reach my goal, but the Lord would not let me become overwhelmed, and always provided me with the strength of a wild ox and of an eagle.

We sent church planters to the countryside of eastern Cuba from 1991 to 1996. They walked through very dangerous places, survived many accidents, lacked food and money, but when they returned, they did it joyfully, having accomplished their mission.

We reorganized the evangelistic crusades in 1997 when we started to schedule and give lectures to church leaders in anticipation of the crusade events. In this way, the whole congregation of a local church became involved. God began to open doors and blessed us. We collected offerings from the crusades that we have shared liberally to advance God's work. The Lord has blessed our finances and we have never lacked money.

We have helped to establish 50 new churches. We praise the name of the Lord for the conversion of more than 50,000

We used whatever transportation we could get.

people in the last 14 years of work. Every single day is a challenge for our evangelistic teams, including our music team Worshippers of the King that the Lord uses to urge other musicians to join this work. They do their best to be real Levites, worshipping the Lord with their lives.

A few weeks before leaving for a crusade at a Baptist church in Moa, I asked my team to consistently get up at 6:30 am to pray together. We got on our knees and asked God to equip us for that week of hard work. One morning, the Lord showed me that to be a worshipper we needed to prepare the altar. I decided to apply that lesson in a literal fashion. It was Sunday morning and we were getting ready to have Sunday school, so I told the team, "Let's prepare for worship by serving and cleaning the whole church, the bathrooms, and the aisles so that everything will be sparkling clean." The whole place looked great! Later on, we gathered for the final prayer time. The musicians testified that they had felt God's presence and that they were then better equipped to help those who came. Consider this idea as just a small way to keep contributing to the work of the Lord.

A different move of God was seen in the evangelistic crusades in Cuba after 2000. A big crusade ministry named "There's Life in Jesus" started to have great impact in our churches. That made us very happy because we started to see the answer to our prayers after so many years of labor. We soon became involved in this ministry. We gladly acknowledge the sacrifice that sister Rebecca Licea and her team have made, and the overwhelming love she demonstrated in this ministry. She was very good at organizing huge crusades all across the nation.

Here I am in the middle of the "There's Life in Jesus" crusade in Sancti-Spíritus, 2001.

God is using the evangelistic teams to restore ministries and churches, and our purpose is to be a blessing to each one. We hope to help every church become effective and vibrant in it's setting, as that is the only way to win Cuba to Christ. Youth With a Purpose Ministries helps individual churches take dominion over their neighborhood for Christ. Please pray that Cuba and the nations will be evangelized, and that the Church in Cuba may go beyond our national borders to other people who will have the opportunity to meet the Lord.

I personally testify that an imminent call to carry out evangelistic crusades is faithful and true. The Lord owns all resources. He is the owner of all the gold and silver. He opens doors and pours out blessings because He owns His kingdom. Men of wisdom and intelligence will never stop evangelizing. Even those who do not believe in God must admit that the Gospel enables Man to develop a better world, and to have stable families full of love. This peace and hope is never a cause for shame, but is the ever-present hope of a Christian.

The musical group *Adoradores del Rey* (Worshippers of the King) plays a very active role in our evangelistic outreach.

8

Evangelizing Children

As a servant of God, I have a passion and love for children that has become a reality in our lives. Soledad and I remember our childhood, and all the sacrifices of love and integrity that our parents displayed; how they taught us to discover the path God had preordained for us, so that once we were old, would never depart from His teachings and will. What effective Sunday school teachers we had! They instilled God's word and knowledge in us.

Unfortunately, children are often considered a nuisance in our churches. When a small child walks up and down the church aisle during a service, I have heard some preachers say, "Brethren, don't be distracted by the devil's schemes that steal your attention." Then, the kids are immediately removed to another room where someone keeps them amused until the service is over. Whoever acts this way has certainly ignored God's plan for children. We have always regretted this type of situation and have long realized the need for trained, full-time workers for our children's ministry. Teaching resources are scarce but we have gradually trained workers and obtained resources for children.

When we began working at the church in Babiney in 1991, there was a group of children who used to upset the rest of the believers because of their misconduct. They were the cause of disputes among the adults, many who did not want these children in their services and events. If any missionary tour was ever planned, these children were the first ones to be sent away. My wife and I determined to treat them like our own kids, and began to disciple them according to their gifts. We formed a choir that was soon invited to sing in many churches. We often held evangelistic crusades on the streets, and these unruly waifs soon became an asset and learned to have hearts for ministry. They were actively involved in the founding of three new churches and twelve missions. I must admit that we suffered a lot. We usually had to convince unsaved parents to allow their kids to attend our events. When their children were sick, some parents would ask us to help take them to the hospital, and we were often requested to intervene in problems at school. I always remember Lelanis with love; as I had to be there for her many times. We were like family to many of these children.

When pastors and adults could not see the vision God had given us for ministry, it was the children who first caught the vision and stood in simple faith. They believed God for the winning of Cuba and the nations to Christ, the School for Church Planting, mass evangelistic crusades and the training and commission of full-time Christian workers. They were always willing and available to carry out whatever tasks were necessary. They never hesitated; on the contrary, they were an inspiration and never doubted what we said.

We have been able to rejoice as these kids have grown into men and women, most of them still serve God effectually and have remained faithful to Christ. Some have completed Bachelor's degrees in Theology; some are completing their postgraduate course at the Youth With a Purpose Seminary. We now have one young man in the Dominican Republic who is pastor of a church and has a wonderful ministry with children. This makes me think of the importance and priority of instilling Christian love and faith in a child's heart. Whoever endeavors to teach a child will not have wasted his time, because children have a special sensitivity to God's voice. Statistics show that those who meet the Lord in childhood are more likely to remain faithful than those that are converted as adults.

After having worked with children for some time we decided to begin the Evangelistic Ministry for Children. Our purpose was to provide a children's training program that would provide child-focused discipleship training over a ten-year period. We systematically presented material while we trained them in the Great Commission. We designed a curriculum of courses based on Bible studies made by other people and their experiences. We adapted each study syllabus for the program; and trained men and women who felt called to do this wonderful work. We provide for spiritual growth by using Biblical doctrines that develop a healthy and spiritual pattern of growth in the kids. It's necessary to train children no matter what the cost. What really counts is that 10 years later they will be the young men and women that God will use to carry out His work. This results in more youthful and vibrant congregations. The church will be infused with enterprising young people who are not afraid of the future, willing to spread the Good News.

I visited my home town in March 2003 after many years. Everything was so different! Many things had changed in 20 years; even the landscape had changed. The whole place was in ruins. The house where I spent my childhood was destroyed except for a few pieces of floor that still remained intact. I found the old corn mill hidden amidst the undergrowth, and the whetstone we used to sharpen our knives and machetes was broken in pieces on the ground. Memories of my childhood came flooding back and I wept. I felt a mixture of pain and sadness, but I also saw something that made a great impact on me: I saw the coconut tree that my father had planted when I was small. Twenty years later, in the midst of all the ruins, facing the deserted countryside and storms without assistance, the tree remained alive and strong, offering its fruit and shade to those who daily passed by.

The lesson that I learned from that visit is that I need to sow into the future. I realized that there is a great problem today. Very few people are willing to work with patience for things that take a long time to bear fruit. The little coconut tree my father planted is there today and it is a blessing to many because of his foresight.

Become a person who plants trees for the future. Even if you are not able to eat of its fruit or feel its shade, what matters is that others will eat and appreciate what you did. I will always be grateful to my God for those that have sown into the future, so that I can enjoy the fruit of their labor today.

We live in a world of instant gratification. We love things that are done quickly, immediately. Our spiritual life is not like that. It must grow according to God's timing. Working with children is like planting a tree. When the seed of the Gospel is planted, it requires some time and attention. Cultivate the heart of a child to be open to God's heart. Children want to learn the truth and they will receive the Word of Truth quickly. Do not refuse to teach them, because they are fertile ground that we are called to help nurture. Guard the hearts of children from the ruin of wild sin offered by the world. When they become adults, they will be grateful to you. Even though they are in a world that is in ruins, they will be equipped to bear fruit. We disciple our little ones, believing that one day God will use them mightily as missionaries, leaders, pastors and teachers. My parents, for example, did not know that they were investing in a child who would be called by God some years later. I want to let children know that they have a part in God's program, and that if He has called them, then no one can stop them.

Our ministry offers support, training and provision (within our means) to help evangelize the children of Cuba. The Redeemer Baptist Church in Céspedes has a building for this purpose. We have men and women committed to working with children. We are a blessed family of believers, sowing into the future and offering a challenge to all leaders and pastors to invest in the lives of every child for the sake of the Gospel.

Children's ministry in Babiney, 1995.

VBS activities, 2006.

9

The Moses Orphans' Program

One day as I was preaching on the streets, the Holy Spirit led me to enter a small wooden house. The place made me feel lonely and sad. It looked deserted, yet there sat a hopeless woman. A 3 year-old boy sat in a corner of the house with no clothes or shoes on. I carried him in my arms and I could see in his eyes how badly he needed to be loved. I tried hard to make him smile without success.

Where are his parents?" I asked. The woman replied sadly, "His father died and his mother abandoned him". My heart flooded with compassion and pain for that little boy's situation. When I returned home, I shared this sad experience with my family and we agreed to buy him clothes, shoes and some food. We also let our church know about it. Many brothers came to my office over the next few days to tell me about other orphans they were aware of in similar conditions. We soon knew of 27 children needing help. This became a great challenge and burden that we didn't know how to face. I found James 1:27 very encouraging. "Pure and undefiled religion before God and the Father is this: to visit orphans and widows in their trouble, and to keep oneself unspotted from the world."

I immediately started to worry about how and where we were going to help them. I brought the matter to God in prayer. I could feel His presence, and I spent some hours telling Him of my worries and my ideas, but at the end, He gave me the answer. He showed me how to put a project into practice to help these children. Every orphan would be taken care of by an individual caring family. We would be the bridge between this family and the resources that the ministry would supply to help meet the basic needs of the child. God has been in this ministry from the beginning and has not failed us in supplying for the needs of the orphans in the Moses Program.

I rejoice when I realize that simply being willing to do God's work was enough for us to receive all kinds of blessings and to be able to help each orphan feel truly loved. We now work with 33 orphans . We are assisted by a wonderful team who loves them; and two of our assistants are Nolaima Amat and Leydys Díaz.

An orphan needs consistent love because he has lost his loved ones. Many of these children have seen one of their parents kill the other. Others may have heard about how their parents died in an accident. Their memories are like a never-ending tragic movie. Only Jesus could give them peace. It is a sobering experience to hold a child who has never known anyone he could call Dad; or to spend time with a teenager who lives every day seeing her classmates share their lives with their parents when she is not able to. There is a void in these kids' hearts that only God can fill. I feel comforted when we love them and are able to provide them with a new family and to help them see God as their heavenly Father.

I encourage every church to realize that there are always needy people around us and God is pleased when we serve them. An orphan is not only the one who has lost a parent, but also the one who does not have a heavenly Father. Both of these orphans need our help.

I want to end this chapter by quoting the words I spoke to a group of religious leaders who were wasting their time chatting about complex ideas and theories in a long meeting. "Please, don't teach me so many theories and empty messages that only show your intellectual capability. Don't waste your time simply talking about your good ideas. Please show me how to put your theories into practice. Show me how to apply the fruit of your ideas."

With my wife, Soledad, and three of the orphans we have helped sponsor.

10

Constructing the Redeemer Baptist Church in Céspedes

Our church building was a dilapidated wood structure, built in 1923. The wood had become rotten and unstable with time, and the floor was dangerously weak. There had been accidents where church members had simply fallen through dry-rotted portions of the floor. It was a common occurrence for people to hurt their legs after becoming trapped between broken planks. We had all kinds of insects and bats living between the ceiling and the roof. Bats would fly freely during the service and sometimes they would even crash into a brother or the preacher himself.

Whenever we started praising or played music, soot would fall from the roof, causing painful irritation in our eyes. When we stood on the platform, it appeared that the whole building might collapse at any time. It was decided that the building had become too dangerous to use, and was actually at risk of collapse. The building had become a point of ridicule and joking throughout the town. The poor condition of the building made us cry and mourn like Nehemiah.

There were many that did not believe that we could build a new church, but our confidence in God comforted us as we sang the beautiful hymn, *How Great Thou Art*! In times of great difficulty in the past, when we were without the physical strength to stand, we had been comforted and encouraged by that song, as we knelt, singing hand in hand. We read Nehemiah 2:20: "So I answered them, and said to them, 'The God of heaven Himself will prosper us; therefore we His servants will arise and build, but you have no heritage or right or memorial in Jerusalem.'" This scripture became a reality to us, as God provided all we needed to build the new church.

He prospered us in many ways as we took on the Nehemiah Building Project.

God directed us to start demolishing the wooden structure on September 28th 2000. The church continued having services in the building we now use for children's education.

The original building, constructed in 1923.

We were told that a short-term mission team from North Carolina was coming on Jan 10, 2001 to help us put up the walls. The foundation needed to be ready before that day. We did not have enough steel rebar to start building the foundation, and this presented a huge challenge. I gathered my construction team on Jan 5 and told them, "We believe in a God of miracles. His Word says that the disciples had worked all night long and caught nothing, but following the word the Lord spoke, when they obeyed and cast their nets they caught a multitude of fish. We are going to catch a multitude of steel."

We also discussed the feeding of the five thousand (John 6:9). I asked, "How much steel do we have?" Someone answered, "Just a small amount." We needed three tons of steel to get started. I said, "We have enough for God to do a miracle." We arranged to meet with all the workers involved in the construction project, along with some leaders and deacons from our church. It was almost 10:00 am. The team asked, "Where is the steel?" I answered, "God is going to provide it." Our faith made it possible. We were able to borrow the steel. Miraculously, the Lord started to provide what we needed just at the right time.

When Brother Larry and his team came from North Carolina arrived, everything was ready. The Lord provided me with key men and women who were strategic in the completion of the project, including José Seota, Enrique Castillo, Armando Amat and Sister Nolaima Amat, our accountant, who carefully managed our treasury. She spared no time or effort in order to support the project. Manolito Méndez provided ice for us each day and Ester Rodriguez treated us to her delicious eastern *pru*, a refreshing homemade cold drink prepared from certain roots. We thank Pastor Alcibiades who was an encouragement to us, as well as our church who committed to pray for us. Sister Teresa Mesa who we called "Tere" was a constant encouragement to me.

Brother Oriol Pereira was very ill, but asked the Lord to allow him to see the construction of the new building. God granted him enough life to see the completion of the foundation and first floor.

What could I say about Brother Pepín, one of the founders of the church? He used to tell me, "I have five prayer requests and one of them is the construction of the new building." I thank Heber Seota whose dream about the sound system came true and Arildo Matos who was vital in making the church pews. Brother Nelson Donet and our secretary Ledys Díaz gave selflessly of themselves during that time.

I would like to express my deepest gratitude to my wife for her work. She took on the gigantic responsibility of construction management responsibility whenever I was not home. The Lord used my kids mightily as they helped me at work. They never complained, even when they had to be briefly cared for by other families in the church. What great cooperation we had! Our women, men, youth and even our children — the whole church community and their families were focused on the calling, as in Nehemiah 4:23. "So neither I, my brethren, my servants, nor the men of the guard who followed me took off our clothes, except that everyone took them off for washing."

I want these words be written in our church books and proclaimed to all the people, our children and our grandchildren. The God of Abraham, the God of Isaac, the God of Jacob, the God of Moses and the apostles, He was with us in this endeavor, and the Nehemiah Project was directed by Him. His power was manifested in His love for His people. No one can deny it. He chose Spirit-filled men and women to lead this work, and filled their minds with His supernatural knowledge to accomplish the task.

Taking into account all the great blessings we have received, I declare, as a servant of the Lord Jesus Christ, that The Redeemer Baptist Church will celebrate this victory with a thanksgiving service to be held every first Sunday of September. "Then the Levites said... 'Stand up and bless the LORD your God for ever and ever: and blessed be Thy glorious name, which is exalted above all blessing and praise'" (Nehemiah 9:5).

During the construction of the church, we celebrated two thanksgiving services and praised God for the miracles He performed during the implementation of the Nehemiah Project. We also bought the truck we used to carry the building material during that time.

We started to lay the roof on Friday, September 14, 2001. It was a rainy day but the Lord stopped the rain until the work was finished. While the men were working, the sisters of our church prayed that it would not rain and that there would be no power blackouts, because we needed electricity for the cement-mixer. These conditions lasted 10 hours. As soon as we finished, it started to rain and the power went out, but everything had been completed.

During this project, we had two periods of fasting and prayer, each lasting for 40 days. They were such a blessing to everyone involved. In spite of the huge building project work that was being carried out, the evangelistic work was not neglected. We were able to ensure that both of these areas of labor were performed at the same time. God supplied me with strength, comfort, and energy to encourage and direct the ministry of the church during the Nehemiah Project.

In early August 2002, we began to prepare for the dedication of the new building. Everyone involved in this great event were quite excited. The festivities started on August 28th and lasted for three days. Just as Nehemiah and the people dedicated and celebrated the wall that the Lord had allowed them to build, so did God's people celebrate in Céspedes. We rejoiced and praised God Almighty for allowing us to build His house and to enjoy the beautiful result. We kept a spirit of thanksgiving and celebration as brothers from other countries have visited us. Brothers from Park Cities Baptist Church and the ministry ICM were used of God to help carry out this work. We have never tired of thanking the King of kings and the Lord of lords for what He had done.

Our majestic new building, completed in August, 2002.

11

International Prayer Center

When I was in Mexico in August 1997 to give a lecture at the Latin American Baptist Youth Confrence, God dealt with me in a very special way. A few days before the Congress began I was invited to attend a leadership training course held by the Lomas Verdes Seminary in Mexico City. At this conference I learned a great deal about the needs for the Gospel in other cultures and nations all over the world. The passion of my heart was stirred as I sensed how this information supported the vision that we had in Youth With a Purpose. Youth With a Purpose Ministries had been formed six years earlier, and its main purpose was to win Cuba and the nations to Christ. In the beginning we were not sure how God would accomplish this vision, particularly since for Cubans travel and contact with much of the world is restricted.

After the Mexican conference, I traveled to the United States. I could not stop thinking about the revelation the Spirit was giving me concerning the nations. As I read the Bible I was struck with Psalm 2:7-8 "I will declare the decree: the LORD hath said unto me, Thou art my Son; this day have I begotten thee. Ask of me, and I shall give thee the heathen for thine inheritance, and the uttermost parts of the earth for thy possession."

I kept pondering over what I had read. I could hear the words "ask of me," "ask of me" echoing in my mind over and over again. A vision for a dedicated place to pray and seek the Lord gradually formed. I made a drawing of the place and named it the International Prayer Center.

The whole idea looked and sounded like an impossible dream. I began to wonder if an International Prayer Center might be centered in Céspedes? I wrote down all that I was considering, and kept it in my heart. I waited eight years to know where and when God wanted me to start it, and finally began to share the idea with some trusted brothers. Praise the Lord! Finally, on October 4th, 2005 we dedicated the International Prayer Center in Céspedes. The Lord had provided us with a place so that the vision would come true.

Today we enjoy the The Redeemer Baptist Church where the Youth With a Purpose and the International Prayer Center is located. The walls are painted with a world map, a map of Cuba, and Paul's words from 2 Timothy 2:1-4:

> "I exhort therefore, that, first of all, supplications, prayers, intercessions, and giving of thanks, be made for all men; For kings, and for all that are in authority; that we may lead a quiet and peaceable life in all godliness and honesty. For this is good and acceptable in the sight of God our Savior; who will have all men to be saved and to come unto the knowledge of the truth."

My hands are represented in a painting, praying and acknowledging God as the only Author of this huge work. My hands join with other hands to help implement God's desire. People have access to a tower where they may pray in private. This place of prayer is open 24 hours daily. What a blessing it is to intercede for the whole world and pray together for every people and nation! I can see God on His throne and working as the great "I AM."

Do not ever think that it is impossible to do something for God. There is always an opportunity for service and use, because we are the body of Christ. I thank God that Cuban Christians are preparing themselves to serve the Lord. We are praying for all men and women who serve God all over the world.

12

One of My Favorite Sermons: Make a "STOP"

As I finish this book, I want to share with you some notes from one of my favorite sermons. I have preached this message for 14 years throughout the provinces of Cuba and in Argentina, Haiti, Mexico, and the United States. It continues to challenge me every year, and I pray it will challenge you:

    We live in a very fast-paced world where it seems that we are all in a hurry. A commonly heard phrase today is, "I just don't have time." We are surrounded by many time-saving conveniences: instant milk, instant coffee, soft drinks and even pre-packaged foods. Men are always trying to achieve bigger goals in less time, looking for shortcuts and the easy way out. It seems that few have enough patience to do things well. Sadly, even Christians strive to achieve maturity and to have fruitful ministry instantaneously, taking God's timing and plan for granted.

    Christians who pursue this fast pace often limit the time that they have to invest in prayer, the study of the Word, and perhaps most importantly, simply taking the time to listen quietly to God.

    It is necessary for us to make a conscious choice to STOP. God cannot use you if you are always on the go and never take the time to listen to Him. Let's look together at some men in the Bible who took the time to stop and listen to God, and the results of their having slowed down for Him.

First: Moses made a STOP at Horeb. (Ex. 3)

Moses was busy taking care of sheep; where his biggest concern was finding pasture to feed them. The Angel of the Lord appeared to him in a flame of fire out of the midst of a bush. Out of curiosity Moses went to look at it and was immediately confronted by the voice of God. "Moses, Moses! ... Don't come any closer." These words probably meant, "Stop." "First take off your sandals, the ground where you are standing is holy." We would paraphrase it like this: "Moses, we need to talk, and I need you to be quiet."

They both talked. God told Moses about His call and how He wanted to use him. Moses asked questions and struggled to comprehend God's will. It was then, in that perfect environment, that Moses understood and accepted God's plans for him. After this STOP Moses became Israel's great leader. God's power was manifest in him during every plague, when the sea was parted, when the manna was given, when water came out of the rock in the desert. He saw God's glory and the Lord used him with great power and authority.

Second: In the year that King Uzziah died, Isaiah made a STOP. (Isaiah chapter 6)

It was a time of mourning and Israel was worried about the King's death and was afraid of future events. (2 Chronicles 26). In the midst of those circumstances, Isaiah made a STOP and went to the Temple. He saw the Lord there, sitting on His throne in all His glory. He realized that God was in control and that he needed God's forgiveness. When Isaiah was cleansed of all his sins, then the conversation started between them, and he heard God's voice and answered: "Here am I, send me."

After this STOP in his life, Isaiah became a prophet who was used of God to communicate God's future plans for redemption. Isaiah clearly described Jesus' birth and death. We can learn from Isaiah's experience that when we seek God's forgiveness, see our spiritual condition before the Lord, or are being prepared to speak on His behalf, we need to be in His presence and in no hurry.

Third: Jesus made a STOP for 40 days and nights before He began His ministry.

He made a second STOP before He chose His disciples, and finally, another STOP before He went to the cross.

His first stop (Mat. 4) was to defeat the devil and start his ministry on earth. His second stop (Luke 6:8) was to choose 12 disciples. His third stop (Mat. 26:36-46) was to face the cross.

We can see that Jesus set an example for us, after every STOP he had great victories, even though it cost him everything to achieve them.

Fourth: Paul had to make a STOP on the way to Damascus (Acts 9). Paul was a conceited and self-important religious person. He was heading for the synagogues with letters in order to arrest the Christians. He was so focused and intent on his self-appointed task that he thought he was doing the right thing. The Lord had a red light for him, that light was so strong that he fell to the ground and heard a voice that said, "Saul, Saul, why do you persecute me?" He answered: "Who are you, Lord"? And Jesus replied, "I am Jesus of Nazareth, whom you persecute." Immediately Paul answered, "What shall I do, Lord?" Jesus told him, "Get up."

Fifth: We are being called to make a STOP today as well. My life has been full of situations where God has brought me to a STOP through experiences and decision making. Some examples of this include when I was called to serve God and not to play professional baseball, when I decided to pray four hours daily instead of watching TV, when God revealed the vision of Youth With a Purpose Ministries to me, when God performed a miracle in the healing of my son, and whenever I needed to make a very important decision.

Actually, each of my STOPS has made a profound difference in my life. They have slowed me down and made me think things over.

God has used the STOPS to shape my character, develop my patience, and show me my mistakes. God has equipped me to pay the price of His call. No matter if I'm the pastor of a church in Céspedes or the president of Youth With a Purpose Ministries, I often realize that I cannot make wise decisions without first getting alone in my office, and sitting — not in the boss's chair, but on the sofa where every one else sits. I'd rather allow the Lord to sit at my desk when we spend time talking. I usually put up a sign on my door that reads "I'm talking with God" so that no one disturbs me during those hours. These are very special moments for me, and I advise every leader to practice making regular STOPS, for he will surely find God's directions on the way.

Dear pastors, leaders and missionaries, it's imperative to make a STOP today and check your ministry, your family and your own life. Consider whether you are pleasing God or if there's something missing. Is there any area that you have not submitted to the Lord? Evaluate whether you are using your time effectively.

Be careful with ministries that promise quick success or minimal involvement, because they will stop you from advancing effectively. Take your time; speak with the Lord in private. He has important things to tell you. Ask God to guide you in the footprints of His call for you.

Normally, when a business partnership is being formed, or business decisions are being made, they are not done in haste. Wise people sit down to calculate risk and consider all related details of any business dealing. Only after all the information is obtained and understood by both sides do they come to an agreement. When it comes to Kingdom business, it is also wise to STOP and consider the information and spend time with the 'other party.'

I know that in my life the STOPS have helped me become a better servant of God!

In closing, I would like to make an appeal to any reader who has not yet come to know and trust Christ.

Dear friend, if you are living according to the fast pace of this life, maybe you have not realized that you are on your way to eternal doom and that you are in need of a Savior.

Make a STOP right now and listen to me. God loves you, He has a plan for you, and He will forgive your sins and give you a new life. If you repent, a brand new day will come for you and your family. Do not miss this opportunity. Pray this from your heart, please:

"Lord Jesus, I repent of the life I'm living and I open my heart so that you can come and become the Lord of my life. I receive you as my only Savior."

Carlos with his wife, Soledad, and children, Carlitos and Lianette. June 2008.

Carlos Alamino may be reached at:

Templo Bautista El Redentor
Calle 25 #211
Céspedes, Camagüey
C.P. 72100
CUBA

csalamino@gmail.com

Youth With a Purpose =

Jóvenes Con Un Propósito =

JOCUP